Dear Dale...

1

Dear Dale...

A Tribute to a Friend

In Letters

And

Photographs

Barbara E. Kompik

Printed 2017, Revised and Reprinted 2019.

Printed by Kindle Direct Publishing Company, A Division of Amazon
Author: Barbara E. Kompik and the Precious Friends of Dale Wayne Kompik II.

Contact Information:
Barbara.e.kompik@gmail.com
231-301-5590
7331 Oceana Drive
Hart, Michigan 49420

Bond to the rest of your family...bind each other's wounds... Let the tears flow...and over time there will be chats, Sunday dinners, old memories and new will mingle and form something God has chosen...

- Marji Triol, Canada

To the folks who gave out of their heart and soul, the words to comfort me in my grief along the way, who let me borrow their precious words as part of this book, I love you forever.

To Tarrah Johnson - Eddy, who lovingly and patiently offered to copy and paste the text from the "Dear Dale" Facebook group to a word document. Thank you so much. You are a darling.

Forward by Wade Schultz

Dedicated to Tasha and Natalie

Our Son: His Life, His Death

Dale is declining, yet they continue to pour medicine and blood products into him in hopes he will pull through. But it does look grim.

We are giving him every fighting chance we can possibly give him. His body remains in a very, very delicate balancing act. It is difficult.

We will not give up until he gives in to the fight and God calls him home.

Please, just know that it is a slow rocking motion as he slips from bad to worse to better and back to bad again. No one can predict what the next hour will bring.

I'm sorry.

Thank you for all your thoughts, prayers, words of encouragement and all you have done for us. We love you.

"Dear Dale: A Tribute to a Friend in Letters and Photographs" is a compilation of what was posted on a Facebook group entitled, "Dear Dale..." that his mother created when her son turned septic in the hospital, fighting to stay alive.

Though he remained in a paralytic state, and remained heavily sedated and could not respond but with faint blinks of the eye, thousands of people around the world stood watch and prayed for their dear friend, Dale.

This book is a tribute to a man who lived his life fully in the 31 years that were given to him, and touched hundreds of thousands of lives by simply sharing a unique unconditional love for his fellow man, and also the love of his Savior, Jesus Christ. Many lives were changed because of this one man and how he dared to live differently. Many lives came to say their farewell to a man who had touched them deeply, and were never the same again.

Foreward

Dale is one of my oldest friends; and given that our fathers were also friends, the precedent is set, in Hebrews 7:10, that we have been friends since long before we were even born (this was a little Bible scholar joke we had between Moody grads). Starting back in high school, when kids start to actually consider, with near infinite naivety, what they plan to do, as a career, for the rest of their lives, I had a pretty good idea, rather early on, that I wanted to be a youth pastor; you know, follow in my father's footsteps and all that, but Dale, though his fervor never lacked, could never quite stick to one plan for what he wanted to do (at least occupationally) for the rest of his life. This attitude, in both of us, prevailed through high school and all through college, for me, two schools and four and a half years, for him... well I think I lost track of both.

I am ashamed to say now that, all through that time, as we were preparing for adult life, I looked down on Dale's lack of continuity of purpose and consistency of vocational and collegiate goals. While I was focused on the job I thought was God's plan for the rest of my life and Dale, from my perspective, couldn't figure out what he wanted to do with his, I missed... almost everything.

Dale was building deep relationships that would last the rest of his brilliant life. While I spent time pursuing my goals and neglecting all the amazing people that God had brought into my life, Dale was nurturing his priceless relationships. At the time, I felt as though I was successful and Dale had yet to figure things out. Now I realize that Dale accomplished so much, of eternal value, in his thirty one years that our heavenly Father decided that it was enough, and that it was time to bring Dale home.

Dale taught me, through his life, that it is the people you commune with that add value to your life, and it is the people you interact with that afford you opportunities to add to this life. He followed in Jesus' footsteps; he always made time for people. Dale had an amazing ability to turn a chance conversation, that might have begun and ended with the mundane and thoughtless "how's it going?" into an in depth, challenging, and sincere conversation about who and how you are, with a man that genuinely wanted to know.

He cared about people, in an active way that was unique. Similarly, (and almost ironically) he also followed in Jesus' footsteps in his love of escaping from the busyness of life, into the solitude of the wilderness. Dale realized and appreciated the need for peace and space; the need to escape busyness in favor of unhurriedness, and I have no doubt that it was during those times that his well was filled to overflowing, from which he was able to give to others so generously.

Dale's death forced upon me the opportunity to look back over his life and realize, beyond the shadow of a doubt, that he didn't waste it, but spent it on things I hadn't sufficiently valued, but whose value is beyond estimate. And as I sit and ponder now, I know that his death, though a tragedy, has caused many like myself to reconsider the value of people and relationships and how every interaction can be worthy of our time if we are willing to put in the care that Dale did. I hate that his body is dead, but I am so grateful for the example he set; and I know that if we can be changed for the better, by being reminded of the impact that Dale's short life has had, then neither his life, not his death, has been wasted.

Dear Dale, thank you for your life and for the exclamation point you put behind it, by living it so fully in only thirty-one years.

- *Wade Schultz*

Wade, Torey, and kids.

The more time passes, the less tears I cry.

Jesus is taking my sorrow and giving me life.

But, oh, I still miss him.

Preface

My Friend, Dale

Friendship is an intricate thing. We form friendships for a variety of reason, often on how we value a person. You befriend someone because they make you laugh and have the same interests as you. Other times you befriend someone because they make you think, and they challenge your worldview. Sometimes you form a friendship because that individual is vulnerable, sharing their struggles and pain. But, rarely in life you meet a friend who has all of these characteristics and virtues. That was my friend, Dale.

Dale Kompik and I met the very first day I showed up for my undergraduate degree at Moody Bible Institute –Spokane. During New Student Orientation, Dale helped lead my freshman cohort and later invited me to a house party that was for new students. When I met Dale that day in 2011, I had no idea I had met a friend that I would talk with every week for four years. I had no idea that I had met a friend who would match my aggression and effort in pickup basketball, football, and ultimate frisbee; a friend who would listen to all of my girl issues (I listened to his too); who would be my research partner and stay up with me all night in the basement of Gonzaga's Foley Library; a friend who would not-so-gracefully lose to me in Blitz, Mario Kart, and almost every Nintendo64 game we played; a friend who would introduce me to my now wife; a friend who would ask me any question on any subject and cared to hear my opinion (and I his); and most importantly a friend who cared about my relationship with Jesus Christ and spurred me on to grow by criticizing my bad choices and encouraging me in my virtuous ones. Dale listened to me and loved me, and I him. Dale saw me as a friend who he was to help grow in virtue, because we had the same common end, God.

Dale and I's friendship can be summarized in one story. Dale and I were both staying in Spokane for the summer of 2014, and he invited me to go kayaking one Tuesday morning. I ecstatically said yes. So, Dale and I set off to go kayak the Spokane River at Riverside State Park. We kayaked, swam, and jumped off cliffs for a solid six hours. Theology, philosophy, relationships, politics, economics, we discussed it all. The day was picture perfect. We arrived back at the Jeep, packed up, and started driving home to get some lunch. Then, Dale started laughing uncontrollably. He was laughing at how red I was, an all of sudden, it hit us. Neither of us used an ounce of sunblock on a ninety-eight-degree sunny day with absolutely no shade in which we were on reflective water for six straight hours. Needless to say, Dale and I both came down with sun-poisoning and were literally unable to leave our basements for a straight week. But, instead of wasting away that week in our respective basements, Dale and I never stopped communicating, and during that time Dale helped me with multiple issues I was facing. Dale helped me process a lot of hurt I was experiencing, while also encouraging me not to be selfish in my relationship with Stephanie (my now wife). Dale cared for my soul and my relationship deeply and continually used biblical principals to combat my selfishness; I only wish he would have cared for my skin and brought sunblock to combat the hot Spokane sun. That being said, ten days later Dale and I emerged from our basement caves finally able to enter the land of the living again. Both he and I jokingly remarked to our friends that we wished time could be turned back, so we could bring sunblock and avoid that horrible pain. But, when I think back to that experience now, I actually wouldn't change a single thing.

[OBJ]The calm before the sunburn. July 9, 2014.

My relationship with Dale is both unique and not unique. Obviously, my direct relationship with Dale is unique to me, but Dale's friendship was a common occurrence to everyone who met him. Dale would talk with, eat with, laugh with, anyone willing to be open with him. This could be seen as he was battling his life-ending bout with pneumonia and sepsis. As Dale went through his many surgeries, amputations, and transfusion, hundreds of acquaintances, friends, and family members posted to his Facebook profile; story after story of Dale's honesty, openness, Christ likeness, and dear friendship. And, Dale's death yesterday only amplified the testimony of his life as a vehicle of God's love in this world. In Dale's death, he is proclaiming life in Christ.

As I contemplate Dale's deep friendship, his ability to listen, challenge, and love, I cannot help but think of the reason why he was such a good friend. The wellspring of Dale's love was the person, Jesus Christ. Jesus Christ is the great and true friend of humanity. Jesus loved mankind as a dear friend. He descended to this world and listened to us. He listened to and experienced our pain, suffering, and desires. He criticized humanity's errors and encouraged us with his grace. And, above all Jesus was willing to die if it meant that humanity, his friends, would live in communion with God again. Dale understood this redemptive truth, and he displayed the faith he had in Jesus both in his words and his actions. Jesus Christ permeated through Dale's countenance, character, and conversation. And, because Jesus loved Dale as a friend, Dale loved everyone as his friend. Christ gave himself to Dale, and Dale gave himself to everyone! And now, Dale is in perfect communion with his divine friend, Jesus, experiencing the very presence of the Triune God. And, at the end of days, God will resurrect his body. For, Jesus as our friend and brother has given all who believe in him his resurrection power.

More than physical resurrection, Jesus will redeem and resurrect our earthly friendships and relationships, so that they too are eternal. St. Augustine taught that Christian friendships are eternal because they are formed in the eternal Son of God, Jesus Christ! Augustine wrote in hisConfessions, "Hence the mourning, if one die…all sweetness turned to bitterness…upon the loss of life of the dying, the death of the living. Blessed whoso loveth Thee God…For he alone loses none dear to him, to whom all are dear in Him who cannot be lost" (St. Augustine, Confessions, Book IV). Jesus Christ, as our friend and our cornerstone, makes our friendships eternal. Ecclesiastes famously states, "And though a man might prevail against one who is alone, two will withstand him—a threefold cord is not quickly broken." A friendship in Jesus is a threefold cord. The love of two friends anchored in Jesus shall not be broken, not even by death! Although times of death are painful, the hope of the resurrection and union with God spurs us on to have a certain joy and peace, for we shall see our friends once again and all our tears shall be wiped away (Revelation 21:4).

[OBJ]

Luckily, I pocket-dialed Dale two weeks prior to his hospitalization. That last conversation we had obviously included us talking about the Detroit Lions, outdoor sports, and craft beer. Dale told me about his new endeavors of starting a business and being more involved at his church. And, after the initial hellos and catching up Dale asked, "So, how are you doing?" I answered about how work was steady and my recent move across the country had gone well, and Dale responded, "Petey, not what have you been doing, how are you doing?" I responded how I was struggling with loneliness for the first time in my life. Dale listened to me ramble on and on, and when I finished he assured me that he had experienced the same feeling before and would pray for me to find peace in Jesus. I now realize that my pocket-dial was not mere luck, but the very grace of God allowing me one last conversation with my friend, one final conversation this side of eternity.

"I am the resurrection and the life. Whoever believes in me, though he die, ye t shall he live, and everyone who lives and believes in me shall never die."

John 11:25-26

Praise be to God for His Son, Jesus Christ! Praise be to God for the Holy Spirit who, with God's Love, seals all those who believe! Praise be to God for the salvation of souls and the resurrection of the dead. Amen!

- *Posted on December 20, 2017 by Peter T. Elliott*

You might have read what I have written about the last year and especially the last couple of months of Dales II life. After having taken time to really dig into the deeper questions of the Christian faith that Dale grew up with, he challenged that faith against the thinking and even complete disbelief of the atheist and other forms of theism. After his re-examination of his beliefs Dale II decided to more deliberately live his life in ways that individuals in the early church might have recognized.

That is, he decided to give much of his time to walking up to people and start talking to them, befriending them, serving them in some way, buying them Coffee , or just listening to them. He'd share his challenges, anxiety, and depression, times when he felt hopeless and how he found the answers to those things in the same place many great thinkers found them: The New and Old Testaments of the Bible.

Some of Dale's friends have decided to honor not just the memory of Dale but the New Man or New Women we become when we ask Jesus Christ into our life. It is this, the re-dedication or maybe better said deeper or more complete dedication of Dale's life that is being remembered. It's what his life became by following Christ's example. Dale did it by actually taking to the streets, libraries and coffee shops where he would talk to people about his life, even his guilt and shame for things that were then forgiven, then the mental burden that was removed by the actions of Jesus Christs and what He did with His life. With that action we are given the chance to start over. Becoming "New Men" and "New Women", no matter what our offense.

PARENTAL DISCLAIMER...Dale did not have any tattoos. For the younger ones...he never had nor would he have ever gotten our permission to have tattoos when he was a kid. But it is my firm belief if you are 30 years old or above, like Dale was when he started to look into this tattoo he was in my opinion finally old enough to make a decision on his own as to whether or not he could have a tattoo but his mother disagrees with that statement. In this case his friends, all over 30 are honoring their friend and pointing to new life available through Jesus Christ with this tattoo.

FYI...it was Dales idea was to have it on the arm where it would easily be seen making it a conversation piece so people would ask what it meant. And with that question he would gladly explain.

Funny thing happened typing this message. I was typing this note in a public library. Somebody asked me what the words were on the picture of the tattoo on Matt Bronson's picture. I asked them to wait a minute while I finished. And as I was typing this note in the library the person was reading the story over my shoulder as I typed. Dale had a good Idea because it caught the person eye. When I finished I got up to explain to the person. They put their hands up and started running away afraid I would tell them more about what they read. It was pretty funny.

-   *Dale Kompik Sr.*

For more information about the tattoo contact Matt Bronson, the photographer, and then for the women's wording, contact Dale's sister, Natalie Kompik on Facebook for the wording of 'New Woman".

I have been praying for you and your wife and all of your family for the last couple months, for strength and love and peace and healing.

I wanted to share with you some memories of Dale:

I met Dale in the summer of 2016, a month or so after graduating from Calvin. I was in a rough season of not having a job and not being involved with school stuff anymore and just being lonely, and it was a season of learning about my own brokenness and how much I needed God all the time. A friend invited me to hangout at the college house one night and, not having anything else to do and craving community, I went. I met Dale there, along with a bunch of other men, and I immediately felt at home in that community. Dale was so inviting and loved meeting new people and he was just such a bright light. I think he was almost always manning the grill, cooking up brats and burgers for anyone because it was his house and he was a servant and a friend of everyone.

I kept coming to those weekly get togethers the next couple of weeks to eat and drink and talk about God and be challenged in our faith.

During this time, I also met Travis Johnson, and my clearest memory of Dale comes from a time when I hungout with just Dale and Travis.

Dale and Travis took me up into their prayer room and we spent some time listening to worship music, praying, reading God's word, getting to know each other more, and sharing what God was teaching us. I wish I could remember every word that was said specifically, but I was asking Dale about what he was currently doing, where he wanted to go, and what God was teaching him. I remember him saying how much he was being challenged at work in the hospital and that God was teaching him a lot.

It was really a joy to be open with Dale and Travis and to be able to listen and pray for each other and laugh and love God.

Dale was really a man after God's own heart and he made sure everyone knew that and everyone felt love and he was always willing to challenge others' faith and to be challenged. He inspired and encouraged me to be more inquisitive, to face doubts head on, and to seek Christ first at all costs.

So, I wanted to share just a little bit of my experiences with Dale and how much of Christ I saw in him!

- *Matthew Bronson*

The Letters

December 1, 2017

Dale I haven't seen you in years but I will always remember your sense of humor, kindness n love for life!! Positive thoughts n love from my family to yours!! You truly are a remarkable person.

-Allison R Brown

I've never had the privilege of meeting your son, but I find you and his story very inspiring. Love you and continued prayers for your whole family at this time!

-Sheryl Hatch Beadles

Dear Dale,

We do not know each other, but you do know my daughter Tarrah. As soon as Tarrah learned of you being in the ER, she asked us to pray for you. I can honestly say that I haven't prayed this hard EVER, as I have for you, and I will not stop. You are an amazing person, and God has big plans for you. I am so happy to be a part of this journey of yours. It has made me realize what is important, and what is not. Thank-you for that. Stay strong and keep fighting. I hope one day our families can meet. Spokane loves you.

-Tina Johnson

Dear Dale, this is a long one...but I'm sure you would expect nothing different from me...

I wrote the first portion of this message to your Sister Natalie, the Sunday after you had entered the hospital .I've been so encouraged looking back and seeing how God has been moving for you before and throughout this hectic time.

"These last two months-ish, the idea of miraculous healing has been floating around my mind and has been heavy on my heart. I kept hearing God repeat "miraculous healing, miraculous healing." Which, shouldn't be so strange, He is capable of that! And I think it's safe to say when God speaks to us, it's always for a purpose. I just wasn't sure what to do with what He was telling me yet.

This morning I woke up feeling frustrated with God and asked Him, "Where are you in all of this?" I heard Him tell me to open up my prayer journal and look at how I have been praying for Dale these last couple of weeks. I've known for a while that Dale had been suffering from back pain and lack of sleep. On the 4th of this month I texted him and asked him how he was doing and told him I would be praying for him. Again, I heard "miraculous healing." So that's what I prayed for. Continuing on through the next week, I had been praying for God to heal Dale's body, unaware of the extreme illness his body was actually suffering from, or would come to suffer.

On Saturday, the 11th, Dale texted me, telling me that he was in the ER and to continue praying for him. Which, of course, I immediately did. The last thing he told me was that he had to get a chest tube in. I prayed again for God to heal his body, for "Dale to make a complete recovery". I continued to pray for the doctors and staff, that they would have quick minds and hands.

That God would guide them through the procedures that may come and to have a quick response to whatever issues may come up. I prayed for peace for you, and the rest of his family, and that God would "surround him with a large body of people to pray for his healing and to love on him." Again, praying for these things completely unaware of the severity of his condition and all that would come in the days following.

I am not telling you any of this to get a pat on the back for praying and I'm not saying that God revealed to me how this will all unfold. I am telling you this to hopefully encourage you. After closing my journal this morning God said, "I've been here all along." Even before all of this was fully made aware to any of us, prayers for Dale's health, for the doctors and staff, and for a body of prayer warriors, were sent up. And that was from God."

It blows my mind that God would use me to pray for you that way, before I even fully understood why I was praying such a bold prayer over you. You had been so heavy on my heart the weeks leading up to all of this; I think I told you that. Now, I see why!

I am ready for our conversations again. I don't think we have ever gone more than a couple of days without talking or at least replying to each other's Instagram stories with a snarky remark 🤣 I always look forward to our conversations. You are caring, genuine, humble, wise, funny, intentional, and intuitive. You always point me back to the tender love of Christ. You have helped me unravel my false ideas of myself and helped to remind me of who I am. You've seen me when I haven't been able to clearly see myself. You have helped ease my insecurities, and you've loved me through them. Your heart for God and to know God is unlike anyone else's. Your passion for Christ is so palpable and alive. I am always so energized and excited to seek God more fervently after our conversations.

Thank you for being silly with me, being genuine with me, and for being a consistent and intentional friend. Thank you for your advice, wisdom, and humor.

I am so excited to hear about all that God has revealed to you through all of this! I have no doubt that He has been showing you Heavenly visions.

I really could keep going, but I'm trying to not bore you and I know you're going to have a lot of reading to do. So hopefully I will be able to visit you this summer and I can just tell you the rest in person.

I'm always praying for you. I will never stop praying for you. You're going to have a long recovery in front of you, but I have no doubt that you will overcome anything and everything that comes your way. You're proving that to be true already. Know that I am more than willing to do anything I can for you and your family during this process. I want to help and support in any way that I can.

I love you so much, Dale!

-Tarrah Johnson

Dalezie!! :) You are gonna have a load of reading to do when you start to feeling better! Just sayin' ☺ I want you to know I've been able to speak boldly about your story, about your peace and about our Jesus. A friend of mine who doesn't yet know the Lord has been keeping close tabs on you since she hears me give updates all the time. Amazing! Keep fighting Dalezie!!! "Be steadfast and immovable"! Can't wait to hear your voice... and that chuckle of yours!

-Heather Blair

Endless prayers from around the world...Build the Kingdom.

-Cathie Swanger Funke

Still praying for you, Dale is in God's hands now.

-Carrie Allen

I don't know Dale, but I am following because he did graduate with my son's Girlfriend. I know a lot of them in that class because he graduated a year before my son also. Plus you have been to our coffee shop and I have followed you with your other books and have been promoting you. As a mother of four boys I have been putting myself in your shoes and know how I would feel with wanting all the prayers as possible.

-Emily Sholtens

Barb and family, Proverbs 3-5-6. Hugs to all.

-Barbara Davidson

Dear Dale, no matter the outcome... GOD WILL BE GLORIFIED! I'm praying and have been praying that your ordeal will bring truth to the lost! What a journey you are on and the people that are on this journey with you... They have been warriors!! This has brought so many people to prayer that probably hasn't prayed this much before. We know each other from Cornerstone Baptist Church. You've always been quite the comedian!

-Christina Powery Hendricks

Are you sure this shouldn't be called "Oh Dale"? We decided if we had a nickel for every time we said that, we'd be rich!" Almost every day since you've been sick, I've pictured you stretched out on my sofa (or sometimes bed where the second tv was) wondering if someone (usually Rachel) would make you a sandwich. We loved having our home be your home away from home- mostly when you went to West Shore but often hanging out with Dan randomly also.

It's been an absolute joy to watch you mature (from afar on Facebook). And of course we'd be remiss not to acknowledge there are aspects of your personality (like the man I'm married to) that will never mature But the critical parts are mature beyond your years.

Stay strong in the Lord- you are inspiring us all!! Can't wait to see that smile again!!!

-Jody Young

Hi, I'm Audrey! I live in Grand Rapids. I went to high school with Dale, and one of our homecoming dances. I hope he won't be mad that I'm sharing our homecoming picture? I have only seen him a few times around town in the past few years, but he always took the time to catch up, and for that, I am grateful!

-Audrey Moloney

Dear Dale, I remember watching the movie 'Elf' with you and Cassie a few years ago. Poor Cassie had not seen the movie and there you and I had it memorized quoting lines...we even sang "baby it's cold outside" like a duet lol! After Cassie left, you stayed at my house for a few more hours. We talked about life's ups and downs, unknowns of our futures, yet God's faithfulness and provision to give us just what we need, at the right moments. You have always had the ability to find something in common with anyone and start a meaningful conversation. I so admire that about you! Always remember God's faithfulness and provision to give you just what you need, at the right moment.

-Emily Sholtens

A Mother's Heart

I am, this morning, wondering when God will finally say for Dalezie, "Enough is enough." And spare our baby boy this extreme trauma.

Maybe that's what we should start praying...to end this battling and bring our Dalezie back to us, alive and awake.

That is my prayer.

The longer this extends, the more afraid of his life I become.

Just waiting for that gavel to hit that says finally, he is gone.

I don't know how I would handle it. Only by God's redeeming grace.

Amen, Jesus. - Mama

It feels very much like we have been borrowing Dalezie for these 31 short years. It hasn't been long enough.

But I am coming to feel, in my mother's heart and soul, that it is true for my two daughters too.

My children have been given to me as gifts to enjoy for only a short time here on earth compared to the eternity that awaits us.

Perhaps that is the reason I hug them and tell them I love many many times during the day, and tell them how precious they are to me.

Call me a doting mother, that's alright. I have no regrets in smothering my children with all the love and adoration I have within me. Eighteen short years seems but a moment that they all lived in our home. I would not trade those years for a million lifetimes.

I need my kids. They are my whole world. I couldn't live without them. Dalezie...Jesus...please keep my darlings safe within my heart, your heart. Hear my plea, please.

Thank you.

-Barbara Kompik

Dale appeared in my life as one of my brother's friends from school and youth group. At the time, five years' difference was an impassable gulf. Several years later, after he had done some schooling and bouncer-ing, and I had come back home from grad school, we got pulled back into youth ministry, helping out with the Cornerstone Baptist Church youth group, which both of us attended as high schoolers.

Dale has been my friend ever since. It has been a decade, and I have only watched him grow in his desire to love God and to love His children more fully each day. I don't know that I have ever met someone who wanted to understand this more than Dale does. I am proud of him and the way he has lived for his Lord in a way that is difficult to explain. He can never read enough, learn enough, meet enough people, laugh enough, have enough deep conversations, have enough of the Scriptures, or discover enough of the story God is telling in the midst of and through His people.

To keep this from being entirely serious, I am also reminded of the first time Dale came back to visit my family's home after he had headed out to Moody in Spokane: in the interim, I had gotten a better job, and we had fixed up the basement rec room that he and I had hung out in so much (and where he had couch-crashed more times than King Solomon had girlfriends). His response, as I best remember it, follows:

"A *new couch*? You put a NEW COUCH in MY BASEMENT? Is that CARPET? WHERE WAS THIS WHEN I HAD TO WALK ACROSS A BARE CONCRETE FLOOR TO GET UP FOR CHURCH? What'll be here the next time I come back?"

Also, back before he left, I was watching a movie in that basement late one night and he tapped on one of the windows repeatedly until I finally looked up and saw his face pressed against the window, grinning like he was auditioning to play the Joker. Nearly ruined an easy chair and a pair of pants when I figured out where that sound was coming from. The next day, I went and bought the thickest black canvas I could find and tacked it up over those windows. I have since gotten married and moved, but that black canvas is still there.

Dale: I love you, brother, and I am so proud to know you and have your friendship. There's always a space on my couch.

-Jordan Racey

Dear Dale,

Where do I begin?? Goodness we have known each other over a decade. More like closer to 2 decades I think! We went on countless mission trips together, spent so much time together with all our friends. I "fell off the wagon" or whatever you want to call it, and we didn't really see each other anymore. But when I heard you were going through all this I thought to my self, man, I wish I had talked to you one last time. I was telling my coworkers about you...and the struggles you were going through. And you want to know how I described you? As one of the best people I've ever known. Yes you are a Christian, but you are one of the least judgmental religious guys I know. And I wish I hadn't "cut you off". Maybe I did it because I was ashamed, because I thought you would say I was "bad". But you wouldn't. I shouldn't have cut off a lot of people but I did because I was ashamed. I pray that you get through these struggles so I can have a chance to un cut you off. Stay strong Dalesie.

Love,

Elise

-Elise Poll Pardon

Dear Dalezie, I am praying for you, darling boy. Every day with you is a tremendous beautiful gift. I love you very much, my only son.

Tonight I dedicated my life, the rest of my days on this earth, to be the kind of mama you need me to be. I don't know what that means exactly, but have given my life to serving you in any way that you need me. I know I cannot do it alone. But Jesus will give me the grace and wisdom to know to do for you on a daily basis.

So, this is my prayer of dedication tonight, December 3, 2017. 10:04 p.m., Butterworth Hospital, Ranuuci House, Grand Rapids, Michigan....

_____

Oh dear Lord. You promise you won't give us more than what we can handle. Not in my own strength for I would surely fail, but in your strength alone. I am completely surrendered to your power, Lord, because I recognize that in my mother's heart and soul, I simply cannot carry this burden by myself. You ALONE know the exact words that my soul longs to hear. There is none that knows me better and knows what I need. I come to you totally submitted to you for my very being and strength. I have nothing to offer you. I lay prostrate at your feet. Dear Jesus. I love the very sound of your name. You speak peace to me, every moment of every day. I dearly, desperately need you,. My breath only comes from you.

Be with Dalezie now in this moment. Please command each cell, each blood vessel, and each organ to do its work in his body for this night. Please give us just one more day to be with our son, alive. I know you love him more than we do, more than we can imagine. Give us just one more day to see your miraculous and healing hand upon him.

I resign all hopes and dreams and purpose that I have ever wanted for myself tonight at this very hour, and give them to do what you want me to do for the remaining days I have on this earth. One purpose that you have given me was to be Dalezie's mama. Let me draw on that and be the kind of mama he needs me to be right now. I will give myself up to it. I will carry it with honor and deep humbleness. With your strength, I will see it through. No matter what it takes, no matter the sacrifice. I am willing to do what you have called me to do this very moment. Nothing more. Nothing less.

Thank you, dear Jesus, for giving Dalezie to me. Thank you for the privilege of letting him grow up with me. Thank you for the person he is, and for who he will be, in your hands and by your power. Thank you for all you have given me. I surrender it all to you... .

I surrender all to Jesus.

All to him I freely give.

I will ever love and trust him.

In his presence daily live.

I surrender all.

I surrender all.

All to thee my precious Savior.

I surrender all.

In Jesus's precious and holy name.

Amen

-Barbara Kompik

Dale,

Gosh dude, this is nuts! I still can't really believe this is going on. I keep thinking back to last Christmas, hanging out at Bookmark, catching up over coffee, talking about everything in life... I don't know what this Christmas is going to bring for you, but one thing I do know is that God is the same God this Christmas as He was last Christmas, and even when I/we don't understand why something is happening, He can be trusted. There's an old song that goes:

God is too wise to be mistaken

God is too good to be unkind

So when you don't understand

When don't see His plan

When you can't trace His hand

Trust His Heart

I was just telling someone at church today that you are one of the strongest people I know, and even in this circumstance you're challenging people. I read the comments, see all the people praying and read about all the lives you've touched in so many different ways and I wonder, 'what would people say about me if this ever happened to me? How many people would come to visit? How many people would say I've shown them God's love or challenged them in their walk?' Dale, even in this horrible situation, God is using you to reach and challenge people.

I really hope one day I can sit across from you, with a coffee in front of us, catching up and talking about everything. That's my prayer and will continue to be.

Love ya friend,

Jenna

p.s. Mike Donehey from Tenth Avenue North knows your name and has prayed for you specifically... I know how much that would thrill your heart because of how excited you get over "famous" people in the Christian music industry.

-Jenna Nelson

Dale is a rare Christian. Love you buddy! Praying non-stop for you!

-Rebecca Hamilton

Dear Dale,

I am honestly not the best for words, but I think back to when I first moved to Ludington 12 years ago and had a hard time getting to know new people. You were one of the first of a few guys from church to befriend me. We have had some good conversations, great memories made, and a pretty awesome friendship. You always wanted to know how God was working in my heart, caring more about that relationship than anything. That has meant a lot to me. As I was out taking photographs tonight I was praying for you and for the people that are being reached through this whole situation. We love ya brother!

-Matthew Bronson

Dale, I'm not sure if our paths have ever crossed over the years but we certainly know some of the same people. I have felt a burning desire to pray for you and your family over the last couple weeks like I haven't felt in years. The stories people have shared and the impact you have had on people's lives is truly inspiring. I am a father of four and I pray that my children can have the same impact on their peer's lives as you have on yours. It seems clear that you truly understand what is important in this life. I will continue to pray that God uses you and your story to draw people to Him while at the same time giving you and your family strength to endure. Rest easy tonight, you are in His hands. His love endures forever.

-Zach Sweet

Good Morning Dalezie! I'm sending you Psalm 46 as requested by my friend Judy and her sweet daughter Grace. They don't have Facebook, but they wanted to send you a verse to let you know they are praying for you! PS. "Very present help in trouble" has also been translated "well proven help in trouble"!! Wow!:)

-Heather Blair

Hey Dale,

I have been sharing information with our graduating class since the beginning, but I have started sharing on my personal page because you would not believe the amount of people who ask about you. You have SOOOOO MANY people all over praying for you. People who have never met you have heard your story and are genuinely praying and thinking of you as if you were family. You are bringing people closer to God and many people are praying harder and more often than they have in their lives.

-Tara Lynne Hartley

Having known Dale for just over 17 years and spending a LOT of hours together in high school and then again after I graduated college... here's a little levity.

Dale and I were part of a crew of roughly 60ish on the Cornerstone Baptist Church youth group's mission trip to the Hampton Roads, Virginia area in late summer 2004. Dale and I had just graduated from Ludington that May.

The trip is a whole other post, but it was fantastic and I still have great memories of it. On the way back home, Dale and I rode in that white Campus Life bus (the Eagle III, I think). It's an experience. Anyway, Dale spent a lot of time in the back where there's an enormous bed-style loft over the luggage section. It was awesome. I rode about in the middle and spent most of it playing cards with Chris Didur or passed out, napping.

So we're headed home were just about to stop for dinner. We're all tired and Dale was about six degrees past slap-happy. And that's when he challenged me to a fight... on the bus.

"Hey Racey..."

"Yo, Dale."

"You should fight me."

"What?"

"Come on, Racey! Fight me!"

Utterly confused, I sarcastically said, "Naaaah."

Dale was unfazed. He bellowed, "Racey, you will fight me!" Then, he grabbed the pillow off my lap (so no more napping) and bushwhacked me with it.

"Wait, what?"

"Fight me, Racey! FIGHT ME!!!!"

"Eh, okay."

And he kept hitting me with my pillow. Over and over and over again he did this, beating me like a madman with the pillow and yelling for me to fight him. Meanwhile, I literally just sat there and let him do it (I was wiped out and sincerely didn't care that he was doing this). Finally, our youth pastor, Jim Schultz, yells from the front, "Tyler...? Dale? Are you guys okay?"

I answered, "He's fine, Jim!"

Finally, after between 10-20 minutes of this, Dale stopped hitting me, and exhausted... fell asleep on the floor of the bus. He didn't move until said dinner stop.

I don't know if that counts as having fought him, but I'm pretty sure I won. Best part: Dale and I continued to joke about me fighting him when he and I both came back home and he'd camp out in my basement.

So that's one facet of how I remember Dale and his antics. Dale is unbelievably hilarious as well as one of the deepest and most sincere/loving guys I know.

Love you, Dale! Honored and challenged by your Godly walk and glad to call you my brother and my friend, man.

-Tyler Racey

Dale it's been years. I have some funny memories with you...like tipping over the portajon in the cherry orchard. Lol. I laugh every time I think of that... My favorite memory though was being set up. You were sure I wouldn't come if you got hurt everyone else was sure I would. You know you were kinda mad that you lost that bet. Truth be told I would have done it for anyone. I consider you my friend...I pray daily for you to heal and wake up. Come back to us Dale. God's not done with you yet. Love and prayers to everyone.

Santana Rennhack Hart MI

-Santana Ann

I pray for this family I know the pain of seeing your son laying in a bed not knowing what will happen next I know the pain of burying my son, I pray dale will get better and rejoin his friends and family amen.

-Christine Fuller DeVries

Dear Dale,

You've always been my reading/blogging friend. Essentially any interesting Christian article I read, I think "hey, I should send this to Dale". It's just always been your thing, and you love writing that makes you think. I've always really appreciated that about you, and really connect with it. About a month ago, I got the opportunity to write an article for a Christian blogging site. My FIRST thought? "I gotta get Dale to contribute to this site!".

Well, now my friend…my first article with them is published. I look forward to sending it to you to get your thoughts, just like I planned to since before I started writing it. I'm missing your posts. Keep fighting, friend!!

-Quinlyn Jackson

Hey Dale!

I don't think we've seen each other since high school (although we talked about getting together a few times when we were both living in GR). I can honestly say you're one of the sweetest people I know. I've never thought any different... from the first time we met - playing badminton in gym class, and even despite the hundreds of thousands of times you felt the need to "hummmm" my name through the halls of LHS... in class... in choir... on FB (lol)...

Speaking of choir, Those are days I surely miss. Especially how lucky I was to stand in front of you for the majority, listening to your magnificent bass!

Even though we haven't really stayed in touch much over the years, I've visited your FB page often to read your encouraging posts. It is quite clear that you have touched the hearts of many.

Thinking of you daily, and looking forward to seeing you at the next LHS reunion!

-Alycia Hummer

Dear Dale,

Remember this day? One of many days we climbed random rock faces. I pretended to be very confident but was actually shaking and afraid of heights. You always made sure the rest of us were safe. We are here for you now. I know you are afraid and confused and maybe even angry. That's ok. We're here for you. We'll make the climb together.

-Katie Barber

Dear Dale,

We put up our Christmas tree tonight. As I re-discovered this ornament, I was reminded of you. I'm including our newest ornament of our Miracle twins. Because God did the impossible in our lives. You'll see how He will in your life, too. Watch and see.

-Becky Young Gerhart

Dear Dale, You may not remember me as our families do not spend much time together. I am your dads cousin, Aunt Marva's Daughter. I feel as though I have come to know you as I read the stories of those that share on their pages, or here in this group. We were up to the hospital and your mom told us how you were a fighter. Boy I can believe it. Wow, what a fight you are in. I eagerly wait for Natalie's post each day morning and night. I pray silently, or out loud. Occasionally I know the spirit takes over as the words do not seem to come from me. This tells me that God is not done with you yet! Our Small Church Home group is praying for you as well as a Bible Journaling Group that I admin. Satan has a way of trying to knock us down, but the Battle is the Lords and has already been won. Lord, be the hands, minds, and hearts of the staff on the fifth floor of the Fred and Lena Heart

Center in Grand Rapids Michigan as they seek understanding and care for Dale. Let their inabilities be Your ability to restore Dale back to healing from the inside out. Every cell, in the name of Jesus heal, every fiber of every organ line up, mind be whole, liver function, heart beat, and lung breathe by the power of Jesus name. You are the same yesterday, today and tomorrow. We know of the miracles in ancient days and we seek you for that same power today in Grand Rapids Michigan. Lord, hear our prayers.

-Paula Meyer

I have so many fond memories with you Dale! One of my fondest memories of you was on the Fall 2009 Retreat to Center Lake Bible Camp. Mark was deployed and I used helping with youth group as a distraction from missing him. You are such a hoot to be around and you helped those lonely months go a bit faster with your humor, talks and the fact that you missed Mark and Matty almost as much as I did I'll never forget it! God's got this, Dale! He's got you and I take so much comfort in that. Praying for you constantly my friend!

-Rebecca Hamilton

Dear Dale, Everyday this kids in 5/6 class at Covenant Christian School in Ludington pray for you. They ask me almost everyday. "How's Dale doing? Have you heard anything today?" We pray for your healing, we pray for your family, we pray for a miracle....everyday. Can't wait to see what Gods got in store.

-Amber Boerema

Thank you for the friend request. I've wanted to send you a message since I started praying for Dale. Every day I've tried to think of what I would say but words fall short. I want so desperately to encourage you, to give you hope and peace, to help you feel less alone and less afraid. I want to say all the right things but it seems, during a season like this, there is no right thing to say. I'm a young mother, one little girl and one on the way, and my heart can't fathom watching one of my children go through what you're having to watch your baby boy go through. And you're doing it with a measure of faith, courage, grace, and love that most people don't even have for their daily life. Watching your family cling to Jesus, run to Him with everything, praise Him unconditionally, and steward this season so beautifully tells me it's no wonder Dale is the incredible man I've heard he is. The way the body of Christ has rallied together to pray for him, the COUNTLESS stories of people whose lives have been touched by Dale.... I've never met him and I know beyond a shadow of a doubt you have a very special son. But I believe this tremendous impact his life has had pales in comparison to the impact his life is going to have. I see him writing books, mentoring young kids, traveling to speak, becoming one of those viral Facebook and YouTube videos that make you go "WOW I had no clue people like this existed... I want what they have. Who is this Jesus they love so much?" I see his life unfolding in a way more beautiful than any of us can yet imagine. I see him not only pulling through this, but coming out the other side better than ever. Like my favorite Beth Moore says, "I'm better off healed that I ever would've been just plain well." I'm in the trenches fighting this fight with y'all, believing for healing, victory, and double restoration for all that is lost in this battle. In the Bible whenever God leads His children into a season of loss, difficulty, and defeat and they steward it with grace and courage like your family is, He always gave AT LEAST double restoration for all that was lost and some times as much as sevenfold. I am believing this for Dale and for your whole family. Until we see that day come, I'm standing with y'all in faith and prayer. Please keep the updates coming and let me know if there's anything I can do from east Texas. Blessings.

-Julia

Dear Dale,

You don't know me, but I sure feel like I've gotten to know you over the past several weeks. Heather Blair and I go to church together. I'm praying for you, and for the obstacles that are in your path. God's totally got this and he has you, too. If there's one thing I've learned about you, it's your confidence in Jesus, your love for people and your giant heart. I'm praying for your family and other friends as well. I cannot wait to say to people,

"Look what God did through my Facebook friend and brother, Dale's life!"
He's close to you. Closer than the air you breathe!

Zephaniah 3:17

"The Lord your God is in your midst; a Mighty One who will save. He will rejoice over you with gladness; He will quiet you by His love; He will exult over you with loud singing."

-Tara Martin

Amazing things are happening Barbara!!! I'm encouraged every time I read posts saying their friends who don't even know Dale are praying! Could we even begin to fathom how many people are out there praying for Dalezie??!!

"We may never march in the infantry, ride in the cavalry, shoot the artillery, we may never soar o'er the enemy but WE are in the Lord's army!"

As they come to mind, can we please have first names of the staff memebers at the hospital helping Dale???

Keep going Kompik family!!! There are legions behind you!!!

-Heather Blair

Dear Dale, did you ever expect that your life would be an inspiration to so many today?? Or have brought so many people to their knees praying for God to heal every single piece of your body?? To God be the Glory!! You are truly a blessing by our Creator who we give all the glory!! I pray for you every day!! To even be featured in a magazine?? I hope to see and read your story in many more news outlets!! I read all day long posts of people who are touched by your life and are praying diligently for healing of your body! Hang in there Dale.. God has you in the palm of His hand still shaping and molding you as He prepares you for your next journey in life!

-Christina Powery Hendricks

Dear Dalez, I have been wanting to write you a note, but had no words; then, I listened to the luncheon graduation speech you gave at Moody. WOW! That was inspiring! You said " The greatest lessons in life have come from plans that have fallen apart". I can't express to you how encouraging it was to listen to your speech. I know you do not seek praise for those words of wisdom, but I believe it is okay to tell you the great respect I have for you. I see the same humbleness in your words that I have seen in your mom's words. I respect your willingness to share your private thoughts that you encountered after being asked to give the speech. Dalez, you had an impact on me way back in your fourth grade Sunday School class. I was the helper then to Amanda Seaver. I remember watching you exhibit self-discipline and restraint to sit still when it seemed like your body was eager to be moving about. It impacted me because I honestly had never seen a child so visibly struggling with sitting still, yet you chose restraint to sit and pay attention. I have shared this with several people over the years, because I really respected that quality in such a young man. I haven't seen you in many years and I haven't been in touch with your family except for Facebook, but you all have a special place in my heart and I am deeply grateful to be a part of the multitude of brothers and sisters in Christ, whom are praying for you. You are inspiring myself and others to be more genuine, to share Christ more, to love in action and to hope beyond what seems possible. Your family has a faith that can move mountains. They not only believe in God's mighty miracle capability, but they KNOW God has done and continues to do what seems impossible. God is being glorified throughout your battle. His name is being lifted high. Even in your rest, God is being magnified. I am so eager to see how God continues to use you. I desperately ask Him to heal your body and to peacefully guide you as you wake up to recovery and rehabilitation. God isn't finished with you yet. He has a perfect plan in all of this. I believe you are a man after God's own heart. I thank God for your humble heart and for the determination he has given you to live life fully with reliance on God. That is the man I saw as I listened to your speech and that is the man I see as I read others words about your character. Continually praying for you and praising God for accomplishing much more than one could ever do on their own. Glory to God! Love and hugs to you Dalez. " I will lift my eyes to the hills; where does my help come from? It comes from the Lord; the Maker of heaven and Earth"

-Tonya Moore Koch

Dear Dale,

I do not know you personally, but when you overcome all you are going through I will drive anywhere to meet you. I ran across your story on your Mom's Facebook page, as we are Facebook friends.

I am praying for you and your sweet family that has been amazingly strong through this and by your side. I find myself signing in to Facebook several times a day to see how you are doing. Thanking the Good Lord after reading each post. Some days are more complications, but from what I see of your life you just keep getting through it.

You have so many followers and I'm sure some are like me and have never met you. But we have grown to love you and pray for you to keep going. I have faith you will as Good has been by you getting you through each step.

For now I'm signing off, but you are always in my prayers as well as your family and friends. There's not a time that I don't think of you.

So, until you get through all of this, I'll be following, praying and waiting to meet you.

Tonya

-Tonya Green Wilson

Dear Dalez,

It's snowing out today. It's a new season. You have made it through Thanksgiving. Now you have to make it through Christmas. Next it will be a New Year. Come on Dalez! You can do it! Love, Mama

-Barbara Kompik

Dear Dale,

I do not know you and I do not know your family, however I have been following your dear mom and now you. I have been praying for you every day along with your friends, family, doctors and nurses .

Sometimes bad things happen to good people, that's what we hear. You often hear, how does it all make sense?

I know because my dad passed away at a very early age, I was 16 and could not figure out why him?

Well, what I do know Dale is that there is a time for everything and everyone. I also know that people are learning about themselves and the Lord through you, that my dear I hope you will always understand, remember and be thankful for.

Your precious mom and family have been at your side, we are all pulling for you.

When you awaken, you will see how much love is surrounding you.
You are in my heart and prayers.

-Michele Gamble-Schaefer

Dear Dale,

I know the fight is difficult, but you are overcoming every obstacle that has been thrown your way. It is amazing watching you fight because you are so strong. I know that with God's help you can overcome anything.

By the time you read this, you will be well on your way to recovery and you will have conquered all.

You have a new life, Dalez! We weren't expecting this, but perhaps God had prepared your heart for such a time as this. You were desperately searching more of God, and I believe he is and will show you now through this experience.

Thank you for being my son. I love you beyond words.

Love,

Mama

-Barbara Kompik

Dear Dalez,

People ask how I can be so strong in the face of this tragedy. I tell you, it is not me but it is God's grace and mercy that people are seeing. It has NOTHING to do with me.

If it was me, I would not be able to look into my baby boy's empty sedated eyes and stroke his hair in undying love.

If it was me, I would not be able to look upon his broken body as they have taken one lung, his two legs at the knees, see his dying hands that he will soon lose, and know they have had to cut his organs out where they have died and are sending toxins into the rest of his body.

If it was me, I would not be able to see the many lines that are inserted into his body for as much life support as he needs to survive this.

If it were me, I would not be able to endure the stress and grief the rest of my family is experiencing.

If it were me, I would not survive the pain of losing my only son.

I think of the story of Abraham and Isaac in the Old Testament. God commanded Abraham to put Isaac, his long awaited son and only child, on the altar to sacrifice his baby boy to please the Lord.

Though stricken with grief, he CHOSE to obey God. As Abraham raised his sword to slay his own son, God sent a ram, it's horns tangled in a bush, to be the substitute for Abraham's precious son. God spared Isaac, and he lived.

I choose to follow God on this life and death experience with my precious and only son. I choose to say yes to whatever God wants to do with my son's life.

"Yet though he slay me, or my son, I will trust in him."

People ask how I can hold up. It isn't that hard. Because it's a choice I've been given. I chose to follow God no matter the cost.

And when I lay myself on that altar, like little boy Isaac was, I know my God will be there with me and my baby boy, no matter what sacrifice he calls on me to give.

You are my all in all, sweet Jesus.

-Barbara Kompik

Dear Dale (or as I like to say Daaaallee!!!),

I saw you on the news while I was in the break room at work today. Dude, it was mad weird....ya know, like that's Dallleee, my gem of a friend who's in a hospital that's a 15-20 minute walk away from me...

I keep thinking of when you unexpectedly showed up at my work back in March and we were both so surprised to see each other. Ha! I can't believe you recognized me but then again, why wouldn't you 😄😂 but I recognized you right away too, so there it is. Those few minutes we talked were such a joy-booster and kinda like old times when we'd see each other out and about in Spokes. Oh Spokane.

Anyway, I've gotten the chance to tell my coworkers, most of whom aren't believers, about you and the stubborn hope I have in God about ya. As I've been sharing updates I've been able to talk about the fragility and strength of life, and also of why I believe you'll pull through.

When I met ya Ma, she said you were stubborn and I told her I am too and that's probably one of the reasons we're friends. ☻ ☺ It's been mad dope to get to know ya fam bam, and they're pretty cool...which is obviously why you're cool (duh). I miss ya, ya little nugget and am praying for you daily, hourly, fervently. I can't wait for you to wake up and all that stuff. I'm not super sure why this has turned into a novel...but then again, I am a writer.

Speaking of which,

I have been writing a lot and I've thought about you often. Thanks for spurring me on to not quit at it...our conversation about it meant a lot. And in case you didn't know, I'm super glad we reconnected fam bam. Welp, I'll be seeing you around GR sometime, I've chosen to believe...(and eventually I'll get to Madcap)

You and ya fam are in my prayers,

-A.A.V.

Dale, (I'll try to keep this one shorter...)

Last night was another really rough one for me. I have moments where I can accept that this is happening to you and trust God regardless, then I have moments of utter frustration and heartbreak. I'm beyond ready for this to be over, for you to be healthy again. I know that my desires and heart for this situation will not thwart the plan that God has for you and I am learning to trust that His plans and thoughts are indeed higher than mine. I am learning what it truly means to have faith in the midst if chaos and it is not fun, nor is it easy. But it's a valuable lesson and my faith is being made so much stronger because of it. I have never sought the wisdom of God so much, I have never prayed so fervently. It's terrible that it has taken a situation such as this to constantly drive me to my knees. I am so thankful for the many ways God has used you to spur a new passion for Christ in me, and this is another one of those times.

I cannot wait to see the incredible ways God will use you in the future. You will continue to touch the lives and hearts of people and impact them in ways immeasurable, just like you have mine. You have been nothing but a constant encouragement, an amazing friend.

I miss your words, wisdom, humor, and conversation.

I will continue to lift you up in prayer and support you and encourage you through your recovery and adjustment to life outside the hospital. You forever and always have a friend in me.

Keep on fighting, Dale Wayne.

I love you more than you know.

(P.S. sorry, I said I'd keep it short, but you know me...)

Also, this is the one and only picture we have together (we will change that someday). You don't even realize a picture is being taken and I look like a complete goof, but it's been a favorite of mine recently.

Okay...I think I'm actually done now...

-Tarrah Johnson

One more light-hearted story from more recent years. When Dale sees or is read this, he'll laugh. And also remember.

Roughly a year or so after I returned home after graduating from Hope College, my Dad had a spinal operation in Grand Rapids. Mom stayed with him, while Jordan and I stayed up in Ludington. It was either late fall or sometime in winter - the snow was flying.

During this time, Jordan got the idea to try an experiment in the kitchen. One of his friends from graduate school days had given him his recipe for homemade spaghetti sauce; this cat is Italian by ancestry and knows how to cook, so we got a good one. Anyway, Jordan decided he and I should take a whack at it with just the two of us at home, and we did exactly that.

Long story short - it was beautiful, if messy. Tomato sauces, for those not familiar, spatter like mad and by the time it was done, our white stove looked like the scene of a slasher film. I had little welts on my forearms from all the sauce that hit me and my shirt had red dots all over it, but we ended up with the base for an amazing spaghetti dinner. The tomatoes reduced nicely, loads of onion and garlic, plenty of cheese, oh, and a couple of browned whole roasts that we shredded. Yum.

Jordan and I can eat well, but all that was a bit much for just the two of us, so we invited some friends over to help us eat it, including our beloved Dale. While we were finishing prep, Dale kept us company with jokes and the like. While he was doing that, Dale noticed the pictures over the mantelpiece, including my old senior picture from high school. When he spotted it, he literally yelled, "Holy *FATNESS*, Tyler!" (I had lost over 40 pounds since then and I look quite different from high school years).

"Wait, what? What are you talking about, Dale?"

"You... your picture... you look so... so..."

"Bigger? I look bigger there?"

"... Yeah. That."

Needless to say, I switched the picture out for my college senior pic shortly after this happened (we *DID* have an amazing dinner and fellowship together, for the record.) But Dale still would occasionally remind me of "Holy *FATNESS*, Tyler!"

-Tyler Racey

Dear Dalez,

I know that your thirst for going deeper with God could not be quenched. You were always searching for more. I believe that God is quenching your thirst in this experience he has given you...and all of us as we sit by and watch. I believe that God will not let his word come back void. I believe he is crafting a beautiful story for you to share within the confines of this world and in the heavenlies. I believe you will speak again, this time uttering the goodness and greatness, and the height and depth of just how awesome our God is.

I am anxious to hear your story, sweet boy. Live on, darling Dalezie!

-Barbara Kompik

It's hard to beat a man who never gives up, Dalezie! Just wanted to remind you, You 1000% have what it takes.

-Heather Blair

Dear Dale,

I want you to know how much I miss reading your posts on Facebook. I've been following your spiritual journey for a while now. I have loved reading about what you are reading, why you're reading it, and most importantly what you think about it. The depth of your thoughts and your desire to truly understand and follow Jesus has been such an inspiration to me. These mornings when I pop onto Facebook and know that I'm not going to see what you are thinking are sad. I hope you understand that even before this journey your life was impacting so many others, and challenging us to keep learning,keep searching, keep caring. I fully believe you will leave that hospital with a greater story to tell, a greater love to share, and a greater impact to make. Praying always...

-Tammy Daggett-Bailey

Dear Dale,

I know it's been years since we've spoke but I wanted to tell you that I still remember the fun we had singing in Collegiates together and I still remember something you told me during a conversation we had online after we both went off to universities. I was talking with you about how I was struggling putting my faith in his hands. I told you that I liked to be in control of my life and making my decisions and you told me this: "Think about this. When you are in control, who are you making God?" That has stuck with me for the past 10 years. Even though we haven't talked since about that time, I have always remembered that comment and to remind myself to let God be in control of my life. I've always enjoyed reading your posts and wish we would have kept in touch. I am continuously praying for your healing and for your family.

-Jenna Stalmack

December 12, 2017

Dear Dale,

I met you at Moody Spokane and you were the kind of guy that always made those around you smile.

I know life moving forward is going to be a huge change. Never forget that God is holding you in his hands and that he loves you so much.

You continue to bless everyone around you just like you always have. Keep fighting the good fight Dale!

With love, Angelique

-Angelique Noël Downey

Dear Dale,

I heard about you long before I met you. Ben would talk about your crazy antics as roommates when the two of you lived together, as well as the long conversations you would have.

I met you in person for the first time at Amanda Visser's going away party before she moved to Texas. You told me a little bit about your life goal of being a physician. More specifically, you chose that path because you felt called to minister to the upper class. You talked about how we as westerners seem to think that only those who go "without" need Jesus, but you said "what about those who think they have everything, but don't?" I'll never forget it. You've changed your path career-wise since, but the overall mission has always remained the same.

From there I'd see you from time to time, usually in coffee shops or at our "family breakfasts." You ALWAYS made it a point to stop and say "hi" with a smile, coupled with a big hug. When I ask how things are, you've always just been honest. It doesn't matter how great or ugly it is. I absolutely love that about you! You never feel the need to cover up with a false facade.

If you're at odds with God, you're real about it. If God humbles you and puts you in your place with His gentle love, you just say it exactly as it is without any shame. SO GOOD!

I can't wait to have more conversations with you and hear about what God's doing. The good, the great, the bad, and the ugly. You are a FORCE, Dale. You are loved beyond measure by so many. Keep staying strong!

~Quinn

-Quinn McGill

Dear Dale,

I'm my lifegroup's Bible study tonight I ran into this verse and thought of you:

"I want you to know how hard I am contending for you and for those at Laodicea, and for all who have not met me personally. My goal is that they may be encouraged in heart and united in love, so that they may have the full riches of complete understanding, in order that they may know the mystery of God, namely, Christ," Colossians 2:1-2 NIV

I'm thinking of how many people you have touched who haven't met you. It's true you are suffering and you have a long road ahead. But how many people have been exposed to Christ through your faith and life's testimony?

-Becky Young Gerhart

I remember just a few months back when Dale told me he didn't like the meaning of his name, which is, "the valley". He said he always thought the valley was dry and barren, a terrible place to be.

I told him to encourage him, that, oh, no; the valley is lush and green, fertile, where a quiet river runs through and strong majestic trees grow, rooted deep alongside the river. A resting place before preparing the difficulty of ascending the treacherous mountain climb that lays ahead.

I think he felt better about the meaning of his name after that.

And I believe with all my heart that he is making that climb up that mountain, and it is rocky and difficult.

I also believe he will reach the top of that mountain with God's strength and endurance, and finally know the height and breadth and depth of God.

.... Dale loves to hike and rock climb!!!!

Go Dalez!!!

-Barbara Kompik

Dear Dalez,

You are my darling boy. You always have been and you always will be.

I remember the first time I saw you. I exclaimed, "what a beautiful boy!!". I was so in love with you. I still love you with that same adoring love that only a newborn baby brings out in a mama.

Oh how I long to hear your voice again. Your laughter. Your beautiful boy laughter. You laughed at everything. You were such a happy boy. Oh how I love you so much.

I remember when it was my turn to be in the hospital two years ago, fighting for my life. I was so sick. And through that experience, you told your daddy that you and I had been best friends during your high school days. You have no idea how completely honored and humbled I was when I heard those words. They meant everything to me. They still do.

I am proud of you, my darling boy. I always will be. You will always be my baby boy, no matter how old you become.

Please wake up soon.

I adore you.

Love,

Mama

-Barbara Kompik

Dear Dale...Last night as I prayed for you and your family I had a moment of anger as I questioned God Why? Not why you because you have always been the "If God brings you to it, he will bring you thru it" type of person. My why? was more, why God are you making Dale go thru this trauma? I had it out with God for a few minutes and then it was as if I heard "because Emily, I want to save him" what? And then I thought maybe... just maybe God has used the doctors and medical people this far and now he wants there to be nothing more they can do so HIS sovereign healing can be the only explanation as to how you go on from here. Come on Dale, Gods not left you he is leading you over this mountain!

Throughout today, I have had this song in my mind when I start doubting what God is doing for you. I hope it helps you on the days you feel your faith being challenged.

"Give me faith to trust what you say...I may be weak but your spirits strong in me. And my flesh may fail but MY God you never will!"

-Emily Scholtens

Dear Dale, You don't know me personally but you know my brothers...Nate & Mike Lipps. I've heard nothing but fun encouraging stories about you. Especially during St.Paul years growing up. Your spirit shines through everyone that has met you. It's amazing the different interactions that I've had with with complete strangers lately and they mention your name. If you only knew that from the North to the South, from the East to the West people are encouraged by your story. You are being the "Light "! How amazing! Our Church family here in Elk Rapids, Mi have been listing you up in prayer. Our immediate family have been lifting you up in prayer. God has you cradled in his arms. You will change this world Dale! God has plans for you. I look forward to hearing about your journey!. You define the term "Salt of the earth"! I leave you with a song that touches my heart. I hope you enjoy.

PS) You have an INCREDIBLE family. They have been an inspiration in themselves. Your mother, father and sister have been by your side 1000% WHAT A BLESSING. I can see how they instilled such a strong Christian foundation in you! They are Soldiers of the Lord....Dale Sr, Barbara, Natalie, Tasha....thank you for all the updates. Your constant faith is breath taking!

-Alexis Manning

My Dear Dale,

Words cannot describe the emotions felt over the past few weeks...and I'm sure everyone can relate to that feeling. I haven't been able to compile words until now, so here are all the words.

I think of the day we met frequently. It was my "unofficial going away" bonfire at Derek's in May/June of 2015. You had just moved to GR and had made your way into our group of friends. I remember you making fun of me (along with everyone else) when I told you I was leaving West Michigan to move back to the East Side for a job and to be closer to my family. I made the trek back to GR a lot that summer, but our paths didn't cross much.

Our next big run in was the NYE 2016 Party at Derek's (anyone noticing a theme here???). Once most people had left, you, myself, Haley, and Derek climbed into Derek's new hot tub as the snow started to fall. I remember you (in your oh so suave voice) asking me if I worked out or did CrossFit, as I had "built and toned shoulders" This sparked a whole new level friendship as I shared with you my love for working out and my career as a physical therapist. From then on, you've never been shy about asking me for rehab help or how to fix random aches and pains! I remember spending four hours with all of you in that hot tub, staying up until 4am that night, thinking to myself "how did I get so lucky to have such awesome friends." I don't even remember what we talked about, but it must have been good if the conversation lasted four hours.

Since then, we've shared text messages and phone conversations from afar, and face to face conversation when I've come back into town. Sharing woes on unsuccessful dating stores and celebration with the good ones. You and Matt introduced the crew to Peter Pan Land in 2016, which I thought was the most beautiful place I'd ever seen until I went to the Pacific Northwest and experienced real mountains just a few weeks after that. You were right, there's nothing like a real mountain! You probably recognize the background in my profile picture. Haley took the photo, but I'm pretty sure you said something to make me belly laugh as she snapped it.

My most recent memory with you is when we walked to the beach from our campsite in Ludington, talking and watching the storm roll in over Lake Michigan. You guiding me in the dark because you apparently have night vision and I apparently do not and sound like a bull in a China shop when walking through the woods. You went through a lot this past spring and summer, both emotionally and spiritually. The depth of your thoughts and feelings blew my mind. I didn't understand some of the things we spoke about, but the way you spoke showed your spiritual and emotional growth and how in tune you are for wanting to always be learning about your spiritual gifts. Whenever I felt like I needed a spiritual pick me up, I knew I could go to your Facebook or Instagram page and be pointed in the right direction. I've had Hillsong's Of Dirt and Grace album on repeat lately, per your recommendation a few months back.

I want you to know that everything that has happened in the past 6 weeks has driven me to take a long and hard look at my life. What I'm doing with it, the people in it, what I want out of it. I'll be honest in saying I've strayed from my faith a bit the past few months. God has hit me hard with realities, I've shed a lot of tears, but through all of this, God is getting the glory. Your story has been shared with most of Southeast Michigan and I'm pretty sure all of IHOP (no, not the pancake house, the International House of Prayer in Missouri) is praying for you. A group of my friends out here are going to donate blood in your honor this weekend, in hopes that it will save a life, just like a random stranger's blood saved yours.

My dear Dale. Please keep fighting. You can and will overcome any obstacle when you pull through this. I've already told my PT pals in GR who work with amputees to keep an eye out for you, that you're a spark plug and an instigator. I came in to town to visit you a few weekends ago, just after the docs said no visitors for you. However, I was able to spend time with your lovely family and our friends. God has blessed you all with such a deep love for one another, and I can only imagine how that love has strengthened. I love you, man. And I'm praying hard for you and for the physicians taking care of you.

P.S. you're welcome for that photo.

-Laura Kordick

Dale, this is a book I suggested to you over the summer that we talked about briefly. It's similar to Scary Close, it is titled The Relational Soul...today I decided to look through it and as I was flipping through I found these pieces I had underlined. I couldn't help but reread them with you in mind. You are an incredible man, Dale!

..."True surrender is not resignation or a passive giving up on life. Surrender is a Spirit-empowered act of courage. It is the willingness to offer our lives to God and trust him with the outcome. It is giving up our lives to God each day, recognizing our dependency on him. It is trusting God even when what we are living is dark and confusing and something we never thought we would have to live.... He was teaching me the craft of being a follower of Jesus... His surrender didn't eliminate his suffering or mine, but his faith held his suffering, and that proved to be part of his surrender to God. In watching him surrender in faith I learned a way of doing the same.

Surrender, even when seemingly foolish, in time forms a quality of life that reason will never find."

I can't help but relate this excerpt to you, Dale.

All of my love to you and your family.

-Tarrah Johnson

Can't help but think about my approach/perspective to praying for Dale Kompik when I read through this. Hope it can be a blessing or encouragement to someone else:

"True intercession involves bringing the person, or the circumstance that seems to be crashing in on you, before God, until you are changed by His attitude toward that person or circumstance."

-Quinlyn Jackson

Dear Dale, missing you today. I love to go to Ferris too. It was a joy, upon entering, to scan the room and find you there "studying" so often. I still love to go there when I can, and I still find myself surveying the space when I walk in to see if there are any familiar faces. praying for God to continue working in your body and mind and that soon I can run into you again and have one of those deep philosophical conversations like we used to. Praying for healing for God's glory and for your good, and so that we can be blessed with your presence again. We love you friend, and we are standing with you.

-Tammy Joy

Dear Dale, I don't have any specific memories to share, only that in high school you were always good natured and wearing a smile no matter what. My favorite part of our high school graduation was the song you performed. It took a lot of courage and strength to get up there and perform in front of so many people. This is the same courage and strength lead by God that is helping you in this fight. Lastly I wanted to share with you some pictures of my son, he is going to be 3 months old and makes the craziest faces. May he put a smile on your face as you continue your journey.

-Nicole Marie Lindenau

Dear Dale,

Please don't go.

Please.

People are waiting with great anticipation to hear your incredible story. You have a mission to fulfill. You can't go yet. Please don't go. We need you very much.

Love,

Mama

-Barbara Kompik

Dear Dale,

Today at work was ugly Christmas sweater day. Although, we have smiles on our faces there was not a moment today we didn't think about you, pray for you and your family, or talk about you. I have a feeling your sweater would have won today. We are missing our co-worker/friend/family. We are waiting for the day we hear you say "How is your heart today?"....

Love,

Your Hope Family

-Shannon Haskins, Brittany Hartman, Marisa Cisneros, Lauren Mack

---

Found this pic of Dale with Rachel Young at Dan and Jessica Young's wedding. Comments from Becky Young Gerhart talking about makeup looking good and Dale saying thanks...LOL. Hope it brings a little humor to your day.

-Jody Young

Sweet Dalezie, just this morning I had the opportunity to share a spoonful of the gospel to a woman at a store. "No one gets to the Father except through Jesus". I gently said. The only reason this came up is because you came up. A woman who may never have the privilege of knowing you personally seeing how you're states away, heard the Saving Name of our Jesus. Praise the Lord for your faithfulness, Dalezie. I'm so proud of you; at this very moment it sounds as though your family has been instructed to gather around you. Consider yourself surrounded by the thousands who have claimed you as friend. I'm praising the Lord you are held so securely by His loving hand. I choose to selfishly continue to hope for a miracle. Jesus be praised! Your friend, Heather

-Heather Blair

Dear Dale, I feel like I've known you forever, yet we've never met. I saw your story on your Mom's Facebook page and have followed daily, a lot daily. Against my own advice to get off the internet and do something outdoors I've been signing on several times an hour. We are all praying for you, the Drs, family, friends, and medical staff. You've got so many following you and praying. I am definitely praying for a miracle. You have such a story to tell and if the Good Lord is willing He will see to it you get to. I am praying continuously as are so many. Just know you are on everyone's mind and in their prayers.

Always Praying,

-Tonya Green Wilson

Dale, if only I could make it to GR to see you and tell you all of this in person. It breaks my heart to know that you may never get to hear, or read this message.

I just want to thank you for being the friend you have been to me. You are kind, encouraging, humble, and wise. You see people for who they really are. You see people as brothers and sisters in Christ. You love them with a love undeniable. I cannot count the ways you have encouraged me and challenged me. Always getting me to see things/life/myself/others from a perspective I otherwise wouldn't have seen. A perspective of more love and more grace. You speak to me so tenderly, just like our Father. Even in your challenging, you are humble. You never speak in a condescending manner, you only speak in hopes that you will see growth in others, that they will fully step into their identity in Christ.

I love how one second we can be having a heart to heart about whatever struggles we're dealing with, then the next we can laughing about silly posts we found on the internet or just giving each other a hard time. You are genuine, Dale. A man of God. Fully devoted to seeing His kingdom come to fruition. You have a heart so hungry for our Father.

I am so beyond thankful for the time you have taken to get to know me. You have impacted me in ways that I can't fully describe. You are are one of my greatest friends.

I pray that you are not done here on the earth. Seeing just how deeply you impacted the lives of hundreds of people, mine included, I know that you would impact so many more.

I know God is good, His plans and thoughts are higher than mine.
I hope you know somehow just how deeply moved I have been by your friendship. Just how much I love you. Just how badly I want you to stay here longer. There is not a single person on this Earth like you, Dale. You truly are one of a kind. I am glad I got to play a small part in your life. And I am thankful for the HUGE part you played in mine.

I'm not sure my heart has ever felt a hurt like this before, yet I still can feel a sliver of hope and peace because of our Father, and I know you'd want me to lean into Him and hold on to that sliver.

Whatever happens to you, I am thankful that regardless, I will get to see you again.

You once told me: "Tarrah, you have imprinted on my soul." Well, Dale.I can surely tell you that you have imprinted on my soul.
I miss you. I love you, always.

-Tarrah Johnson

For my Dalez,

Dalez, in the last few years of his life, deeply, fervently, without reservation, yearned to know God, not in the usual Christian way, but in a way that pushed him into the depths of realizing his own weak humanity needing the sheer moanings of his spirit to deeply bond with his Creator, Savior, and King like no other. He truly had a hunger for God that simply could not be quenched here on earth.

I believe Dale's heart was in such a state of yearning, that God could not adequately answer his longings without taking him home to be with Jesus in all his glory.

Soon, Dale will see the glory of the Lord that he longed for. He will see Jesus. And we who are left behind will remain in our own sleepy states who can not begin to comprehend the height and breadth, and depth of the glory that Dalez is about to experience for himself.

Bless you, Dalezie, for blessing us with the fullness of your life. We will dearly miss you.

Thank you for being my baby boy and allowing me to see you grow up to be the godly man that you are. What a precious gift you have been.

With all the love in my heart,

Your mama

-Barbara Kompik

God is our help. He is our VERY present help.

Right now, so many feel like the earth we know is giving way, like the seas of life are vicious and roaring.

When this life's troubles rage and our world is set on edge or totally flipped upside down, we know that our God, the God of Jacob, is our strong fortress. He is our very present help, and we look to His mighty power for a mighty miracle.

Psalm 46:1-7

"God is our refuge and strength, a very present help in trouble.

Therefore we will not fear though the earth gives way, though the mountains be moved into the heart of the sea, though its waters roar and foam, though the mountains tremble at its swelling. Selah

There is a river whose streams make glad the city of God, the holy habitation of the Most High.

God is in the midst of her; she shall not be moved; God will help her when morning dawns.

The nations rage, the kingdoms totter; he utters his voice, the earth melts. The Lord of hosts is with us; the God of Jacob is our fortress."

-Quinlyn Jackson

Trusting in God's power to heal you today!

"So that your faith might not rest on human wisdom, but on God's power."

1 Corinthians 2:5

-Rebecca Hamilton

Today's Verse of the Day from the Bible App. I created this image in the app and the caps are my emphasis. I take great comfort in this, and I'm leaning into and asking for God's great power and outstretched arm to touch you, my friend.

"Ah, Sovereign Lord, You have made the heavens and the earth by your great power and outstretched arm. Nothing is too hard for you."

Jeremiah 32:17

-Becky Young Gerhart

Dearest Dale,

Man, am I thankful that I have met you. Even though it was only a couple months ago, you my friend have made a huge impact on my life more specifically my outlook on life and my faith. I couldn't have picked a better person to start my journey at Hope with. I could always count on you to help me look like I was busy when we couldn't find anything to do. The last time I saw you we spent the whole day together in a training. I honestly don't remember much from that training besides laughing and talking with you. I did have to tap you a couple times to keep you awake, little did I know the battle you were already fighting. Thank you for lending me your sweatshirt that day because I was so cold and the sweet smiles you flashed. It's hard sometimes walking around remembering conversations we have had in that specific spot. I wish this journey at our new place of work could have meant more laughs and figuring it out with you. Thanks to you I think I have a new summer hobby in your honor-if only I could get a hold of the designs you showed me so often for the logo.

Always in my heart and on my mind.

Yours truly,

P.S. I will never forget to clock in/out thanks to your sticky note at my desk

-Marissa Cisneros

Dear Dale....

Lauren Macke, my kids and I went to your favorite coffee spot today after attending your church service. I know the doctors are saying one thing right now and you keep beating the odds. You have proven you're a fighter... whatever Gods plans are for you Dale, just know we feel your everlasting presence. We promise to continue to serve our patients the way you would want us to. We will preach the word of Jesus and share your stories. His arms are around us and you my friend. I posted on Friday I wanted to hear you say "How is your heart today", I felt you ask me today by the sign in my coffee and Dale my response is: my heart is at peace today. My heart knows that no matter what happens your story will continue.... God has you.

-Shannon Haskins

Dale, I'm finally starting to read another one of the books you suggested to me. #obvithinkingofyou
I'm choosing to find joy in the little things and in my community and in our Savior Jesus. I know that's what you'd want for me, for all of us.
Coffee-ing for Dale.

Still praying for you and your family, dear friend.

-Tarrah Johnson

Dear Dalezie, I am praying for you, darling boy. Every day with you is a tremendous beautiful gift. I love you very much, my only son.

Tonight I dedicated my life, the rest of my days on this earth, to be the kind of mama you need me to be. I don't know what that means exactly, but have given my life to serving you in any way that you need me. I know I cannot do it alone. But Jesus will give me the grace and wisdom to know to do for you on a daily basis.

So, this is my prayer of dedication tonight, December 3, 2017. 10:04 p.m., Butterworth Hospital, Ranuuci House, Grand Rapids, Michigan....

Oh dear Lord. You promise you won't give us more than what we can handle. Not in my own strength for I would surely fail, but in your strength alone. I am completely surrendered to your power, Lord, because I recognize that in my mother's heart and soul, I simply cannot carry this burden by myself. You ALONE know the exact words that my soul longs to hear. There is none that knows me better and knows what I need. I come to you totally submitted to you for my very being and strength. I have nothing to offer you. I lay prostrate at your feet. Dear Jesus. I love the very sound of your name. You speak peace to me, every moment of every day. I dearly, desperately need you,. My breath only comes from you.

Be with Dalezie now in this moment. Please command each cell, each blood vessel, each organ to do its work in his body for this night. Please give us just one more day to be with our son, alive. I know you love him more than we do, more than we can imagine. Give us just one more day to see your miraculous and healing hand upon him.

I resign all hopes and dreams and purpose that I have ever wanted for myself tonight at this very hour, and give them to do what you want me to do for the remaining days I have on this earth. One purpose that you have given me was to be Dalezie's mama. Let me draw on that and be the kind of mama he needs me to be right now. I will give myself up to it. I will carry it with honor and deep humbleness. With your strength, I will see it through. No matter what it takes, no matter the sacrifice. I am willing to do what you have called me to do this very moment. Nothing more. Nothing less.

Thank you, dear Jesus, for giving Dalezie to me. Thank you for the privilege of letting him grow up with me. Thank you for the person he is, and for who he will be, in your hands and by your power. Thank you for all you have given me. I surrender it all to you...

I surrender all to Jesus.
All to him I freely give.
I will ever love and trust him.
In his presence daily live.

I surrender all.
I surrender all.
All to thee my precious Savior.
I surrender all.

In Jesus's precious and holy name.
Amen

-Barbara Kompik

Dalezie!!

Thank you for being the best teacher on prayer. I better understand WHY we are to pray without ceasing!!

Real quick...when we say we are willing to pray for a brother in need, what we're really saying is "I'm will to go to war beside you." When the enemy or the situation seems hopeless, it is then when brothers and sister around the world are most needed!! The ones who don't even know you or I or your family. To me, it's as though we are fighting this "battle" and all of a sudden a whole new wave of fresh, strong believers appear and are ready to help! Dalezie that gives me goosebumps and hope!! Today that "New Soldier" was made known to me from a friend of a friend. She's 90 years old and serves Jesus with everything! She's praying for you by name. I don't know her but I was so encouraged by a poem she loves. She's fighting for you Dalezie. Through the sorrow, Esther clings to Jesus too! I hope this gives you a boost!!

Thank you to all who both know and have never met our Dalezie!!
-Heather Blair

2:25 a.m.

Tuesday

December 19, 2017

As I lay my head to sleep

I feel as though

I can hear a choir

Of heavenly angels

Ever so faintly

Away beyond the sky.

They are proclaiming

Dalezie's arrival soon.

It is a constant stream

Of high and low sounds

Mingling together.

A never ending praise

And worship

Of Jesus in all

His glory.

Dalez walks steadfastly

And boldly

Towards the choir.

And then he steps up

Into the ranks

Of angel singers

And takes his

Baritone place

Within them.

He is home.

Sing, Dalez, sing.

- Barbara E Kompik, mother of three beautiful babies. I am blessed.

Dear Dale,

You were an all inclusive kind of guy. Didn't matter the event, who was allowed, what was going on - if someone wanted to come you would invite them. Since I've been back in Grand Rapids you invited me to countless bonfires, coffee dates, and music sessions.

My first memories of you involved your willingness to take a Michigan homesick girl on late night walks in a new town where she couldn't venture alone. We bonded and defended our Michigan roots, almost annoyingly so.

There are so many feelings, and words about your passing. Joy that you are with our savior. Sadness and grief that I will no longer sit across from you drinking coffee, and bouncing between serious life talks and light hearted laughter. I will miss you. I do miss you as do so many others.

Thank you for shining so bright and letting Jesus permeate your life. I can only imagine the joy and peace you feel now, and am grateful you have finally arrived my brother.

-Micaela Wire

Dear Dale,

I did not get to know you for long, but when I moved to Ludington and started hanging out with Jordan and all of his (and now my) friends, I found that this mysterious Dale character, and his goofy exploits, were in all the good stories. Your reputation preceded you. But as I heard from the many stories, and later saw from meeting you after you returned from Washington, you were a guy who loved your friends deeply. And I so loved listening to you and Jordan spend a few hours talking theology, the couple of times I got to listen in.

I'm so thankful that our paths crossed, and I'm praising God for the impact Dale has had on me, my friends, and so many others.

I don't have any pictures of Dale and I together, but here he is from our wedding photo-guestbook.

-Katie Nelson Racey

Dear Daleo,

I am happy you're in the arms Jesus now after such a difficult and painful battle. I know and remember a great man of God who showed compassion and had an inspiring wit about him. I am privileged to have known you, looked up to you, and I will always be your brother in Christ. Thank you for the impact you had on me and so many others. Love ya man, I will see you again someday!

Nato Potato

-Nate Martin

I tear as I hear this. I wish I had been a better friend. I hadn't seen Dale in person in over a decade. Someday, Dale. Someday.

-Joel Arvey

December 20, 2017

Dear Dale,

About a year ago we were out to breakfast after I had finished a night shift and we were swapping stories. You were telling me about how you had been eating in the cafeteria on your work break at the hospital and a man at a nearby table started choking on his food. You jumped into action and began doing the Heimlich maneuver. You saved that man's life. I think its clear that you have had part in saving so many more throughout your lifetime.

Thank you for being incredibly goofy, yet also incredibly real.

Thank you for being a friend to everyone...I'm pretty sure you had friends in every age range.

Thank you for not missing my wedding, "for anything in the world."

Thank you for being the man that allows us to know without a doubt that you are singing among angels right now.

-Bree Lauber

Barbara Elaine Kompik, Dale Kompik, Natalie Kompik, Tasha . The first Christmas without your loved one will be hard. You may not feel like celebrating, you will cry and think of the empty seat beside you. May you light a candle in his memory and start a new tradition in his honor. Be Blessed and find rest in the peace of our King Jesus.

-Paula Meyer

Dear Dale,

I recently realized that you were the first person to introduce me to Nordhouse dunes during a youth group camping trip 7 years ago. Since then, I have gone on countless Nordhouse trips and moved to Washington to enjoy even grander adventures.

This summer, at Bree's wedding you were so excited to share with me some of your favorite hiking trails in the PNW.

Thank you for continuing to inspire all of those around you to experience the outdoors. And thank you for showing me that we can experience God and all that he has created on the highest of peaks and the sandiest of campsites.

-Emily Norlund

"Your name, Your name
Is victory
All praise, will rise
To Christ, our king
By Your spirit I will rise
From the ashes of defeat
The resurrected King, is resurrecting me
In Your name I come alive
To declare Your victory
The resurrected King, is resurrecting me"

Elevation Worship

-Karalee Bradshaw

Dear Dale,

I do not have any stories or photos to share, as we had never met. However, I feel compelled to tell how deeply you have impacted my life. When I found out about you being in the hospital, my daughter asked my family and I to please pray for you. We had no idea at that moment, just how sick you were. We thought you had pneumonia and that it would be a short stay in the hospital. Then is when for me, personally, my relationship with the Lord became stronger. I was brought to my knees so many times, praying that God would heal you, so I could have the chance to thank-you in person, but God had other plans. I see now just what that was. I may not be able to thank-you in person here on earth, but I will have my chance when I see you again in Heaven. My thoughts and prayers continue today, tomorrow and always for you Kompik family. Thank-you for sharing your son & brother with us,and allowing us to be a part of Dale's journey. We love you, and are still hoping and praying our families will meet one day.

-Tina Johnson

Dear Dale,

I can't imagine the ache in the hearts of those who knew you because there are thousands who never had the privilege, yet feel such a deep sense of loss. Many are mourning the loss of brother, son, friend... and many are grieving the fact that we will never get to meet this incredible man whose life we'd become so invested in.

I want you to know that, for months leading up to hearing about you, I'd been doing some pretty heavy wrestling with God, specifically about why He allows bad things to happen to His most faithful servants despite great faith and unrelenting prayer. I still don't really have the answers I'm looking for, but I can tell you that watching you and your family steward this tragedy with unwavering adoration for and trust in Jesus has brought a peace to my questions. I'm learning that logic may not go this far, that faith may be all we really have for these questions. So I choose to believe that He took you home because it was best for you, for your family, and for everyone involved. I choose to believe that He allowed these 6 weeks of suffering to bring together an army and create something beautiful. I choose to believe He is as heartbroken as your sweet family and is crying with them just as Jesus wept with Mary and Martha over Lazarus. I choose to believe that He is good, even when we don't understand. And I choose to believe that one day in heaven we will all reunite and praise Him with full understanding for how this all played out.

Thank you for being the incredible man that you were. And I want to thank your family for allowing so many strangers to watch them carry this burden with so much grace, for giving us a front row seat to their faith, and for setting the most incredible example of pursuing Him no matter what.
I can't wait to meet you, brother.

-Julia English

On this day, 10 years ago, my dad went in for quadruple bypass surgery.

The day before I had arranged to take all three of my college exams early so I could get down to Muskegon in time to meet my sister's flying in. I was a mess but as usual, I kept it all inside and was doing a pretty good job holding my emotions in.

I was scared of all the unknowns and what ifs that had suddenly come up. I had to stop at Meijer before driving down. I had a couple random things to get for my mom and I prayed as I walked in "please God help me not see anyone I know"

As I was nearing the checkout area I heard "Hey, Emily how's it going...are you ok?" It was Dale . It took all of me not to start crying right there. I hadn't seen him in a really long time yet I proceeded to tell him what was going on. He listened for a minute or two and then just leaned in and gave me the biggest hug. I told him I wasn't ready for God to take my dad and it wasn't fair all this was happening right at Christmas time.

I lost it crying for a minute then Dale said some encouraging words but the thing I remember every year on this day is what he said at the end. "If God

Wills something, we can't argue or fight him. You just have to pray thru that trial." I remember feeling upset and dumb founded by his response. What did that mean?

He asked me for my phone number to check in the next day. I remember thinking oh he is just being nice. The next day Dale was 1 of 3 people who text me throughout the day to check in on how I was and my dad.

I am so glad God didn't answer my prayer to not see anyone I knew. I needed to see Dale that day and hear what he said.

Ten years later this doesn't seem fair now that Dale is the one gone. He was such a good guy, God honoring man...or maybe it is fair that God has rewarded him to be in Heaven for all has done in his short life!

I pray those words he said to me give you peace and hope this Christmas to "pray thru the trial" you are facing.

-Emily Scholtens

Sing with the angels, Dale!

-Linda Holden

When I think of you, I think of the choir years. How we were both titled "the trombones" of the group because of our strong, clear, and LOUD voices. (Probably why Ms. Sopha always paired us together for song practices lol.)

 I never minded: we would just make faces at each other when she wasn't looking just to mess the other up. Brat. Lol. I think about How bright red you'd turn and smile so BIG when she would excitedly SQUEAL and cup your face in her hands when you'd nail the low notes.

Recently I've been gaining spiritual strength from the sermons and pictures you would share. So often the message or words were just what I needed to hear at that exact moment. I was always so grateful them. I'll miss them and the man who posted them. You have ALWAYS been a source of light for the people around you. Whether with your humor, your kindness, or your spiritual wisdom. I feel honored to have been bathed in that light and to have known you. Rest in peace, my brother in Christ.

And to his family: my heart breaks for the struggle you were put through before your loss. But rest easy knowing you WILL see and hold your son again! You did such an amazing job raising and loving him. He will be missed by many. God bless you and fill you with peace and strength.

-Jillian Carrol

Dale,

It's hard to find words to express what your life meant to me. I guess I can find words, but I feel like they aren't enough. So much has already been said. And I feel like your impact was even more special and more profound on my life than the words I've seen can really explain. The more I think about it, though...the more I realize that maybe the words DO explain how special you were. Sure, everyone is sharing the words...but that's because you were special enough that nearly EVERYONE who knew you experienced you investing in, learning from, and conversing with them on a really deep and meaningful level. SO many people have words to share about you. How did you impact so many people so deeply? The magnitude at which the words are shared doesn't take from their meaning. It adds to it! Everywhere you went, you dug in and somehow also spread out to reach more and more people. I am so very blessed that I was in reach of your spread at a couple different points in my life.

Thanks for being my youth leader, mentor and big-brother figure back in the day. Thanks for asking questions that challenged me to grow in my faith...and for talking me through my decisions about where to go to College. Thanks for insisting that I at least visit His House at GV. Thanks for all of the talks, advice, and care over the years.

And thanks for moving back to GR a couple years ago so I could get to know you in a totally new context.

I always knew you were a great big brother friend, but you were also a great regular 'ol friend (OLD friend, I would probably clarify, as we visited this topic often. :b).

You were one of the best, Dale. Thanks for sharing time, your hearty laugh, your bear-like hugs, conversation and everything that came with them. It was a great, big blessing. I do and will miss you.

-Quinlynn Jackson

One of my friends passed along these photos to me and I wanted to share. These photos are the beautiful sunrise and sunset from the day Dale left this earth. I already love watching sunsets (as I'm not a morning person and am never up for sunrises) but now I will always remember Dale Kompik as I watch the beauty unfold in the sky each night. It will be your light shinning down on all of us asking us how our hearts are that day.

Dale I have just been picturing you up in heaven on a big fluffy chair with your leg a crossed your other knee with a cup of coffee in your hand sitting next to Jesus looking down and talking about all of us. I wish I had the pleasure of having a cup of coffee on earth with you but look forward to the day we meet again and I can listen to all the things you have learned and can teach me. Rest peacefully.

-Lauren Macke

DEAR DALE.ALTHOUGH I HAVE NEVER MET YOU I HAVE LOST SOME PEOPLE IN MY LIFE. THE ANGELS THAT HAVE WATCHED OVER ME AND CONTINUED PRAYER IS WHAT HAS GOT ME THROUGH LOTS OF SAD TIMES. MAY GOD LIFT YOU UP ON EAGLES WINGS AND GIVE YOU PEACE AND ALL THE GREATNESS THAT IS IN HEAVEN.LOVE YOU MY BROTHER IN CHRIST.CAROL.

-Carol Vogl

Dale today is hard buddy. I tried to workout, I tried to clean, I tried to do anything but think of you, but today, I can't. I miss you terribly. I think of all the adventures we had together. All through Ludington, Scottville, and Pentwater. Then to Grand Rapids, Spokane, and somewhere random else in WA! There's too many to count. So much to remember. I looked up to you in so many environments and on the same note was equals as I grew up. My favorite memory of us hands down was visiting you at moody. We hadn't seen each other but once I believe over that first year of you there. I told you how sad I was we didn't end up doing that together. How much better off I thought I would have been doing if I went with you like we planned... But you were right, I walked the road I needed to. You had amazing friends there, they put me up and I loved them like you instantly.

You took me on my first cliff jumping experience!! 50ft of pure adrenaline rush!! You told me to jump and I had no hesitation. "if Dale can do it I can do it!" I remember thinking that as I ran to the edge.

Buddy.... DK! As I always called you. I wish we had more time. The years we had could never be enough. These past weeks have been the first time in the history of ever I have cried over and about you. You were always smiling which in turn meant I was. Always laughing, which meant I was. Always loving, which meant I tried too.

I will never stop caring and remembering. Never stop honoring the catalog of memory's all about you. I will always love you dearly. I'll try not to keep crying to much, I can't taint how perfect the memory is with that kind of pain and sadness. Bedsides, you would tell me to "buck up ☺:)"

Dale for a 31 yr old stud!! (You know) you have left a legacy uncommon of those your age. My only regret is that this message didn't get said to you while I could talk with you. RIP DK!

-Jessica Braun

Dear Dale, I have been searching for the words to say and the prayers to pray since you went home to be with Jesus. You were a man of great respect and somebody that God made stand out among the rest. You are no doubt one of Gods best, and for whatever reason He decided that you needed to be in heaven more than you needed to be here. I will miss you my friend and I am thankful that I got an opportunity to know you.

When I first met Dale we had a good laugh because we were older than most typical Moody students. Was great for me because not all the old man jokes went in my direction. He always seemed wise beyond his years, but he also had quite the sense of humor and the ability to fit in with just anybody he ever met. Not to mention he could grow a pretty amazing beard. I had a lot of respect for this man, and I'll never forget the last time I spoke with him probably about 10 weeks ago now and I asked him how he was doing. He said he was doing great. He was sitting in a coffee shop talking to someone about God. Of course he was. Dale's faith was amazing and He loved God with his whole heart. He is no doubt enjoying to kingdom of Heaven right now as he stands in the presence of Jesus Christ.

-James Taylor

You were, without doubt, Gods finest.....

-Angela Smallegan

Dear Dale, You didn't know me. It is sad that you passed but you went to be with the Lord.

My late husband is also with the Lord. Will you please tell John that Trina said hi. I will be able see him again and I will be able to meet you.

I know your family is hurting but with the help from the Lord they will get through this. Rest in Peace.

-Trina Mauldin

My Dear Dale,

I'm sitting at my desk at work, supposed to be going through patient chart reviews (I'm incredibly behind on patient documentation, per usual), but instead I'm scrolling through your Instagram posts. Your words are beautiful. Your photos are beautiful. You viewed ordinary things as extraordinary.

I am so, so, so sad I cannot attend your memorial service this weekend. But I know you would want me to be with my family. And to inspire them this Christmas season, just as you inspired so many every single day of your life. I was in anguish making the decision to travel to visit family in PA instead of to Grand Rapids, but amidst tears and praying to God to make the right decision, I felt this peace and I knew you were with me. Thank you.

Dale, I miss you. You continue to touch the lives of many. I share your story with my patients. I had one of them pray with me this morning in my office, while I was releasing their psoas muscle on my table (you remember when I did that to you?) So. Stinking. Cool.

-Laura Kordik

I keep thinking how a lot changes as time goes on. Loss is a particularly hard change. I feel that loss knowing that you are no longer in this world. I'm thankful that I do know that you followed Christ and have been welcomed home as a good and faithful servant. I look forward to when I join you and all those who follow Christ in heaven. It's strange remembering a time when I didn't look forward to Jesus' return. I now look forward to it everyday; as we age as Christians the hardships in this world make us yearn for Heaven.

In heaven that we can be fellowship fully. Looking forward to this time sobers me in this world as well. Losing more and more of those we care about also leads to this anticipation. This anticipation should be used to inspire us. Life is brief and God is working, we just need to be aware enough to be a willing part of that work.

You were a part of that work and Good will continue to use you even after you have joined him. You were always a genuine. I really appreciated seeing this on Facebook over the years since high school. Genuinely seeking truth and answers. Many people just give up; seeking can be difficult and the answers God shows us take time.

I always felt encouraged in my faith when I saw your faith in your posts. I could see Jesus through your questions and statements. You were one of our youth group friends that I could pray about with gladness. I was so thankful to be able to thank God for your continued faith and to pray for strength. I saw these prayers answered as you cared for this world but were not of this world. Jesus cares for this world. Dale, you, cared for this world without being dragged down by it's tempting pull.

It seemed like such a long struggle in the end but I'm happy that God was there all along. I'm happy that you are with Jesus, free from suffering and struggle. I'm sad to have the place you ministered to in my life empty but I'm thankful that I know God will fill it up. I look forward to the day when we can embrace once again as friends. I am thankful for the grief I feel in your absence, it is a gift of God. To know that God used you to impact me and others. To know that my yearning for the peace that comes from the absence of sin in this world encourages me to press on toward the goal for which God has called me.

-Mitch Moore

My Son's Obituary

Dale Wayne Kompik II

May 8, 1986 – December 19, 2017

Kompik, Dale W. Grand Rapids, MI Dale Wayne Kompik II, 31, died Tuesday, December 19, 2017 after complications caused by pneumonia. His life was characterized by generosity, a passion for caring for others, and seeking after God. He could often be found talking about life and the Bible and theology at coffee shops around town, turning strangers into friends. He also loved being in the outdoors, camping and kayaking.

He was born May 8, 1986 in Lexington, KY, the son of Dale and Barbara (Sothman) Kompik. He graduated from Ludington High School in 2004 and then from Moody Bible Institute, where he studied Biblical Studies and graduated in 2014. He has called Pentwater, Ludington, Spokane, and Grand Rapids home.

Dale is survived by his parents, Dale and Barbara of Pentwater, MI; his sister and brother-in-law, Tasha and Will Oltman of Grand Rapids, MI; and sister, Natalie Kompik of Grand Rapids, MI. He is also survived by both of his grandmothers, Zora Kompik of Pentwater, MI, and Jean Sothman of Clarinda, IA, as well as several aunts, uncles, and cousins and many friends.

The memorial service celebrating his life will be held on Saturday, December 23 at 2pm at The Point Church (3449 76th St. SE, Caledonia, MI 49316). In lieu of flowers, the family asks that you consider donations to The Acton Institute where there will be a chair in their auditorium in memory of Dale, or to Bethany Christian Services to serve children in need of adoption and refugees in the community.

To donate to The Acton Institute, send checks to The Acton Institute, 98 E Fulton St., Grand Rapids, MI 49503, designating that the gift is for Dale; to donate to Bethany Christian services, visitwww.bethany.org/support-bethany/give/give-today. Funeral arrangements by Stroo Funeral Home.

Published in Grand Rapids Press from Dec. 23 to Dec. 27, 2018.

A New Year

<u>*January 1, 2018*</u>

I don't think there are clocks or time as we know it in heaven but what a glorious way to spend the New Year... forever in the presence of our Lord.

-Jody Young

Below is a photo I took at the end of our blood drive at Cornerstone Baptist Church in Saturday Dec 30. The MI Blood employee is counting and categorizing our blood donations and putting them in coolers for transport. MI Blood's official goal for our drive was to collect 25 units. I decided to be ambitious and set the goal for 50, which was exactly the number of appointments we originally had. We came together and collected 55 units! I found time to sit at the canteen and talk to people that I knew and introduced myself to people I didn't know. I asked those once strangers: "How are you connected to Dale?" I met people who drove up from GR, people who had never actually met you but were inspired by your story and struggle, and people who knew you and wanted to give back because that's what you would have done. The MI Blood workers even know your story. One lady worked other drives that people showed up for and said "#IstandwithDale. Another employee lives in Traverse City and picked up the shift last minute because he was so moved by your story. When I thanked him profusely for coming he said, "It's my privilege to do this. I'm happy to be here." I watched all day as MI Blood employees and our donors enjoyed each other's company while moving through the donation process. It was beautiful.

Here's what I've come to believe through your struggle: Blood supply should never dictate one's medical care. Certainly not when it is avoidable and there's something our community can do about it.

So, I had the idea of making 2018 a year of recurring blood drives at Cornerstone Baptist Church in Ludington in memory of you. I figured this was a tangible way we could continue to remember you and contribute to your legacy. Selfishly, it was a way for me to deal with a world without you in it. Your friends, their friends, and their families are eager to continue donating. Do you realize we had entire families donate on Saturday? Couples, parents and adult children, siblings, and friends using the buddy system (i.e "let's donate together")? Everyone I talked to liked the idea of setting up more drives.

I really like how MI Blood donations stay local/regional. Our 55 units we collected will likely go to supply hospitals right here in West Michigan. Blood supply during the holiday season is critically low, and our recent cold weather has depressed donor turnout at most drives (the exception probably being ours in Ludington). At our drive, people who had to cancel either found someone to donate in their place or contacted me and I was easily able to book their appointment with someone who was there. I made 5 appointments for people for the Ludington Hospital's upcoming drives. All of those efforts will go to help fellow Michiganders, maybe even someone we know.

Donating blood takes an hour of time and can save up to three lives each time. It's relatively easy, and we can all spend time together as a community. We can talk about life, faith, and about you. You would probably have liked what we are starting here. Even though you are not here on earth anymore, your influence is still bringing people together to help others. Through our tremendous loss, others in Michigan will surely live.

-Becky Young Gerhart

January 3, 2017

Dear Kompik family, my brother posted this, and as I read it I thought you might find some comfort in it.

"He giveth more grace when the burdens grow greater,
He sendeth more strength when the labors increase;
To added afflictions He addeth His mercy,
To multiplied trials, His multiplied peace.
When we have exhausted our store of endurance,
When our strength has failed ere the day is half done,
When we reach the end of our hoarded resources
Our Father's full giving is only begun.
Fear not that thy need shall exceed His provision,
Our God ever yearns His resources to share;

Lean hard on the arm everlasting, availing;

The Father both thee and thy load will upbear.

His love has no limits, His grace has no measure,

His power no boundary known unto men;

For out of His infinite riches in Jesus

He giveth, and giveth, and giveth again."

Annie J. Flint

-Tyler Mitchell Eskovits

January 6, 2018

Well hello there! Missing your smile and contagious happiness! Just wanted to check in and let you know I have the honor of taking your office at work and to keep Jenny in line I vow to always rate lunches with Jenny and play her songs that you thought would cheer her up!

Think about you every day! Keep an eye out for us! MISS YOU DALE!

Your friend and coworker,

Marissa

-Marissa Cisneros

Janurary 19, 2018

It's hard to fathom it's been a whole month since you left this earth to walk with God. The sunrise was gorgeous this morning, and I know you had something to do with it. (Would be a better pic without things blocking it, but you get the point.) I had a dream about you last night...you were walking around showing us your healed feet, and while visiting together, you asked if I would go get you some food. All you wanted was a hot and ready and some crazy bread...surprising, I know. When I came back with the goods, the look on your face was priceless as you opened up the pizza box. It was a short dream, but it was so good to see you. Missing that smile and infectious laugh of yours.

-Liz Vander Zouwen

January 24, 2018

Today, I caught a glimpse of a man, standing in the lobby talking to a group of other men near the end of our school day. He bore a striking resemblance to you, Dale. I caught myself staring at him, watching his body language and the joy that emitted from him with which he spoke. My heart wrenched for a moment. Then, as quickly as I could, listened to my spirit and gave thanks to God for having the privilege of knowing such a great man. I know you're rejoicing in the total comfort and endless love of our Savior. Miss you, Dale.

-Melody Pitman

January 24, 2018

Thought about you today, Dale. Comforted by knowing your cheeky grin is practically eternal now.

-Christina Jackson

January 25, 2018

Dear Dale,

I remember walking past you when you were reading your Bible with some guys in a local coffee shop. When my boyfriend came to pick me up, you immediately got up, ran to him, and gave him the biggest bro handshake and hug I have ever seen. After being introduced, let's just say that I never entered that coffee shop without being greeted by your same great smile and your Bible open in front of you. You always asked about how my week was going, but one thing was different - you always genuinely cared about my response.

So thankful for the chance to not only meet you, but to spend time with you and our friends over coffee, breakfast, worship, fellowship countless times during your life here on earth. It is true that God calls His best home first. What a great blessing for you to be dancing with the man you modeled your life so wonderfully after! Love ya, bud!

-Kristyn Lynn

January 31, 2018

Hello Dale! Got to have another wonderful conversation about you with Brooke today. She talked about how much you love Jesus and how you told others that Jesus loves them too. Your impact will never stop with Brooke! She also said "We don't have to pray for him anymore right mom, cause he's in heaven?" I told her no, but that we can still pray for your mom, dad and sisters. She then asked what your sisters names are and when I told her, she said those were pretty names. Thanks again for being our hero! Miss you buddy!

-Rebecca Hamilton

Your legacy is not going away anytime soon my friend. Every day God has been using what God taught me through your life and everyday I ask how's my heart.

-James Taylor

February, 2018

Oh Dale, had a dream last night I was going for a jog and you sprinted past and yelled "slowpoke" with the biggest smile. Not just standing for you, pressing on in this race for you, too.

-Christina Jackson

February 15, 2017

Dale, I was just looking through our texts from the 4th of November. We were talking about how last year was a year of high highs and low lows for both of us and you sent me Romans 5:3-5.

"And not only that, but we also rejoice in our afflictions, because we know that affliction produces endurance, endurance produces character, and character produces hope. This hope will not disappoint us, because God's love has been poured out in our hearts through the Holy Spirit who was given to us."

How good is God!? To put it on your heart to share that with me just a week before you went into the hospital. It's the last piece of encouragement you had for me. Thank you for your reminders, even today. You are a sweet, sweet friend.

Miss you, weirdo.

-Tarrah Johnson

I am lost between hope and grief;
Breathing petitions
And prayers
To hold in my breaking.
Thinking of
All the "could be" in his life,
What might be upon his death;
And
What it looks like, in this waiting.

-A.A. Vincent, *for Dale (DWKII)*

Dear Dale... Love, Mama

The sun is out, and my Dalez is SHINING in heaven today!! Wish I could be there with you, bud, but I guess I've got work to do here first....

That's my thought today anyway.

I took a nice hot bath and got all cleaned up. sweatshirt and shorts, in flip flops. Open the doors! Turn off the heat! Spring is arriving!

And the boys are coming next month already to help finish the porch and build a simple pergola! The time is almost here and I am so anxious!!

The two books about Dale are ALMOST finished! I'm anxious to send them to the printer. Thank you, all, for your patience waiting for them. You are precious!!

I'm like, I can't join you yet, Dalez, but soon, when God calls me, too. In the meantime I shall live the life I've been given.

And that's enough.

I feel as though a book someone was reading to me about me has closed, and a new book is being taken off the shelf and it now is beginning to be read of me about my life now.

Not a new chapter.
Not a new page.
But a new book.

My life with my son was the first book; the new book is life without my son.

They are two different lives and one does not overlap the other.

Just as spring is arriving with th The sound of my Dalez's silence is deafening.

How am I going to survive this excruciating pain within my very soul?

Jesus, hear my groanings. I lay prostrate before you, unable to lift my head and heart in praise. I am overcome with deep, deep sorrow.

I am SCREAMING inside!!!

I want my Dalez!!!

This is more than brokenhearted.

There is no word for it....

Total despair.

Dalez has gone away from me for an extended vacation. I don't know when I will see him again, but I will see him again, one day. Some day.

And it will be in a place where bright white sunshine shines forever and ever. It will be in a place that no one has ever seen before with the naked eye, and it is unimaginable.

Jesus can't let me see him right now because he is working in me about things I need to learn without my Dalez. Secret things. If I had my Dalez, I would never know these special mysteries about God.

And Jesus really, really wants to share these things with me.

I could quit. I could give up. I could completely shut down.

But I would not see the gems of truth that fill my soul and longings.

I must go on.

Dalez, I know you are waiting just for me to join you. And I believe my place at the feast table is right next to you, with little Gracie on the other side.

Babies, wait for me! I love you!

I picture my Dalez in heaven, surrounded with Light that permeates everything there. Everything sparkles. The colors are unbelievably vibrant.

There are streets of shimmering gold, curved in gentle hills with mansions spotted here and there that are more glamorous and beautiful than the most expensive mansion on earth.

These mansions are built with precious gemstones of ruby, sapphire, amber, pearl, emerald, and the vast array of God's collection.

Dale's mansion is built around one of the largest rooms in heaven. He invites everyone there to come visit, and the angels gather around and lead the singing and praise that he accompanies with his heavenly guitar.

He laughs easily, just like he did here on this place. He is so joyful. His smile is infectious.

He simply is.

He is glowing in Jesus's white light robe.

And he is barefoot.

Live, Dalez! I miss you like unbelievably. But someday I will join you.

I can't wait.

It has been said, to live and not be loved is the tragedy of life.

But I say:

To live and not have loved at all is the worst tragedy of all in this life.

Someone near and dear to me asked me,

Is that all you do is write?

I answered 'yes'. But that's not completely true.

I do the essentials of life....

1. Write my heart out every day

2. Live my life in a constant attitude of prayer

3. Constantly immerse myself in Christian music and sing

4. Sit in my rocking chair to meditate and listen to God

5. Then, and only then do I take care of the distractions of life, I.e. dishes, cleaning, and cooking.

That, my friend, is the summation of my life...and I am content.

In one day, barriers that I have lived with all my life have been broken.

In one day, I have found freedom from legalism.

In one day, I have been changed.

In one day, the debilitating fear is gone,

In one day, I have stepped out of my comfort zone into the Light.

I'm so glad I don't have to live under someone else's expectations of me.

I am free!!

Here are a few of the things I learned today with the boys, Dale's best friends...

1. Love has no barriers or requirements

2. I can still fit in with the younger crowd even though I am 30 years older than them

3. That I am freer in Christ than what I have ever imagined

4. Rigid rules are not my style

5. Real men do cry

6. Denominational religion can be a barrier between believers.

7. I can be a loving surrogate mom and grandmother to many

8. That Dale lives on in everyone's lives

9. One man can, indeed, make the world a different place to be

10. I can be as young as I want to be

11. Though we have so much in common, everyone has a life much different than mine, and that is ok.

12. There is a much different, and probably stronger emotional bond between a group of men than there ever can be in our woman's world.

13. Given the right environment, men will express their love and emotions with more credit than what we give them.

14. Men's love runs incredibly deep. That they need the fear of rejection to be gone so that they feel safe to express that love.

15. I can loosen up and be free of rules and expectations and still be 100% acceptable to Jesus

16. Being judgmental towards others stunts a person's spiritual growth dramatically

17. Loving unconditionally is the only way to love

That's enough for now...

A very good day today with the boys!

And, I have made a few life altering decisions for the better because of these incredible men, Dale's best buddies.

Thank you, Darlings.

Matthew Carroll

Matthew Bronson

Bill Pirkola

Wade Schultz

Evan Allen

Graham Crackers Allen

Mark Hamilton

Dale Kompik Sr.

We missed you, Matthew Bronson!!!

We love you guys!!

Sometimes it only takes a moment in time to know someone's soul.

When challenged regarding Christians " marking their bodies" I wrote:

Dear Amanda, I used to believe that too, but was brought to my knees by this holy expression of love, not only for Dale, my son, but also for Jesus. It's a permanent declaration of these men's commitment spiritually. To deny oneself of that freedom in Christ, is....well, defeat unto legalism. These men's hearts are as pure and loving as I have ever seen in my entire life. No judgement.

This song, which was played at Dale's celebration service, is touching the depths of my soul today.

The tears I shed today are of a deep, deep longing for my son back, even though that cannot be.

Once again, I bend my heart to accept the gift God gave us, in this baby boy, Dale, and to ultimately give his life over to Jesus in humble obedience.

His life was not mine to hold close for myself. No, this boy's heart and life was meant to be shared by many, kids and adults in his backyard and hometown even to the far ends of this earth.

Dale's dad and I have been asked to let go and let the world share in the message Dale brought to everyone that knew him, and that is to yearn hard after the Father's heart and to be shown the glory of the Lord so intensely that he was willing to die to this earth in order to experience it.

So many countries were praying for Dale to survive the great illness that he fought. Today I learned that Bulgaria was one of them. Also, there were folks in Africa, Australia, Austria, China, Japan, England, and perhaps others, that were praying for us and him as he battled three strains of the deadly sepsis.

It is my belief that Dale's message transcended past denominational, cultural, racial and gender barriers. His message was so real and transparent that God used him to touch thousands, perhaps millions, on a global scale.

My question remains:. Who was this man, my son?...Some called him a walking angel among us, perhaps a sort of prophet of modern times.

You can't just suddenly stop thinking of someone you love that you not ever physically see on this earth again. So don't ask me to.

The experience was horrific. Not a quiet slipping away, but decisions out of the ordinary were put upon us to try to save our baby, but helped to no avail. Terrible, horrible decisions.

We were best friends. What mother can say that about their sons? I knew this boy like the back of my hand. We were connected.

We stood by his hospital bedside for six weeks, watching him fight for his very life.

We had pressure from one set of doctors to pull the plug already. They were impatient with us. They couldn't understand why we would want to keep him alive.

But they didn't know our boy, how special of a man he had become to literally thousands around the world. He shared his love for God and his fellow man with everyone he met. He had an insatiable desire to know God's glory.

If you can come close to having a child like that be ripped from you, then you may tell me not to think of him.

But I think that would be an impossibility.

I can only

Rest

In my God's

Grace

And

Wisdom

For I

Know

No other

Way

To give up

My baby boy

From

This earth.

I think it's going to be a good day...the sun is shining, I'm continuing to work on proofing the next book...and Dalez is at peace.

So am I.

Dear Jesus,

Keep my babies close by.
Thank you.
In your hands
And in your presence.
Amen

The more time passes, the less tears I cry. Jesus is taking my sorrow and giving me life.

But, oh, I still miss him.

My Dalez...
He was chosen over me to go to God's Kingdom.
And that is all it is.

Hey, Dalez!!!!! (I am shouting now)

What are you doing right now anyway???

What am I missing that you already have???

Oh, boy, buddy boy, I sure do envy you! I'm pretty jealous. You've reached the life you had always dreamed of...and more.

I could never ask you to leave that place and come back to me... But still, I want you, Dalez. I want you.

It's kind of a lonely place, without my son. I don't have anyone else to talk to like my Dalez. He always listened to me carefully. He welcomed a two-way conversation. He gave me his thoughts when I asked for them. He analyzed and translated my words into something he made sure he understood.

He listened ...

And we talked.

I miss you, my buddy boy.

We had a connection unique to just us two. This new normal cannot humanly be reconciled. The mind cannot conceive it...until it happens to you.. and only Jesus can replace the deep deep void that exists. The good part is, God's grace IS sufficient the very moment we need it. It's the only way a mother's soul can survive that special bond breaking, dying.

"Process"... "As a new normal"...my head cannot wrap around those two terms....

Maybe those aren't the words for it .

I cannot "learn" to live without my son. He will, in this life, ALWAYS be gone from me. I don't know that the soul of a mother ever can know anything different other than the truth:. He is always going to be gone from me. My baby....

No, you never learn a new way of living. It will always be severed, broken. You cannot substitute another thought, principle, mode, philosophy, or way of life.

It is a burden a mother carries for the rest of her life. And it's a lonely existence.

A promise of new life,

waken from a cold earth

and warmed by the sun,

so is God breathing new life within me.

Me, before with my son.
And me, after without my son.

It really cannot be any other way.

Breathe on me,

oh, Breath of Life.

And I shall live.

Like a calm.

Like everything is in its place.

Peaceful.

Not sad or tearful.

He's home now.

I was very selfish with my son; I wanted him all to myself. I hated seeing him walk through our front door into the sea of people he was impacting, without realizing what his life was about. I relentlessly tried to keep him home with me. Little did I know that he was turning strangers into family for us before he left us.

May.

I will bury my son in May. When the spring showers bring May
flowers. When the grass is growing green. When the sun shines longer and
brighter. When the robins return and their singing fills the air.

When everything is beginning to wake up to warm breezes When new baby
animals are being born.

The season of Easter and new life.

I shall bury my son in the midst of it all.
And I will bury the burden of sadness.

And I will remember.
I shall never forget.

Dale Wayne Kompik II

Born: May 8, 1986

Reborn unto eternal life:

December 19, 2017

Tuesday, 2:00 p.m.

Dear Dale...

Although the pain seems too great to bear, who am I to question the sovereignty of my Almighty God? Only he sees his perfect plan unfold within our little lives and his plans are always, without fail, the very best for us.

And I trust him.

It still hurts. The pain of not having my Dalez is so real. But with God, I am an overcomer. In his strength, I can do this, for it is only in his strength can I survive such a blow to my soul.

Only in your strength and by your power, dear Lord.

I see you holding my baby in your hands, cradling him with all the tenderness that exists in heaven and on earth. He is in perfect, absolute perfect hands.

What more could I ask for?

I know my baby boy is in your ultimate care, taken out of my hands and placed in yours forever.

My heart will ever yearn for my baby son, and I will forever dry the tears from my eyes from sobbing in the night and in the day.

But it is your presence I long for more than anything, and anyone. Only you can satisfy my soul. In you will I trust.

Selah.

Going Home...

Dale Kompik II, '14, age 31, December 19, 2017, Ludington, Michigan.

Dale made national headlines after he had a lung and both legs removed in an attempt to stop the spread of sepsis. Dale succumbed to the illness, passing away a few days before Christmas. Before his death Dale's repeated prayer was, "Show me Your glory." As a tribute to Dale, those words now title the book, Show Me Your Glory: A Mother's Cry for Her Son, written by his mother, Barbara Kompik.

In life, Dale actively cared for the people around him. In his local community, he made efforts to reach out to the homeless by collecting resources for homeless shelters and connecting with others. He frequented local coffee shops where he would discuss intricate questions of theology with friends. When on his own, he could be counted on to befriend a stranger. He also loved God's creation and often enjoyed outdoor activities with friends, including hiking, kayaking, and camping.

Dale attended three colleges before settling at Moody Bible Institute in Spokane. He graduated with a degree in Biblical Studies in 2014. At a graduation luncheon, he gave a speech about his time at Moody and the future. "We must hold our plans with open hands," he said, "and trust that God knows what He is doing."

Dale is survived by his parents, Dale and Barbara Kompik; sisters, Tasha (Will) Oltman and Natalie Kompik; and grandmothers, Zora Kompik and Jean Sothman.

Obituary in the Moody Alumni News, Moody Institute, Chicago, IL.

The Photographs

Family Always: Natalie, Tasha, Dale

Always silly.

Dale, Matt and Lindsay Bronson

Macho man on the beach at home

Wade & Torey Schultz, Liz Van Zoulen, Matt Carroll

Best buddies, Dale and Matt Carroll

The many faces of Dale

He was named "Dalez" by his sister, Tasha, when he was born. She was three years old. Her name is Tasha LaShay and she christened him "Dalez LaWayne". A friend had called his dad, Dale, Dalez, and it just stuck. Like Billy is to Bill. You can't just call a baby "Dale" without adding a "z" at the end!

Matt Carroll, Matt Bronson, Mark Hamilton, Dale playing around.

Dale, Matt, Matt, Mark

Awww, the beach life…

"Over the river and through the woods … "

Dale and Jeremy Petrous

Best of the best: Matt Carroll, Dale, Bill Pirkola

Dale and Jordan Racey

Mark and Rebecca Hamilton and Kids

Evan Allen, Matt Carroll, Bill Pirkola, Dale

Bestest friends forever and ever:

Tasha, Natalie and Dale

Epilogue

I can't believe it.

I don't know why God does what He does.

I don't know why Dale got sick all of a sudden. I don't know why we were all told he was going to die 5 weeks ago and then we all went on a insane rollercoaster of ups and downs. I don't know why for 5 weeks it felt hopeful, like there was no way he wasn't going to make it and then everything took a turn for the worst.

I don't know why God took Dale today.

What I do know is that Dale put up one hell of a fight.
What I do know is that Dale is no longer suffering. He's in paradise, embraced by His Savior.

In his last weeks on this Earth, Dale's impact on this world reached thousands of people. He has always had an impact on people. He was intentional and transparent. We had countless conversations about his struggle with depression and I was able to share about my struggle as well. He always had an ear to hear and wisdom to share. He was eager to learn and to share what he was learning.

I want to share a funny story because there are a lot of nice and beautiful things to be said about this humble, truly Jesus reflecting man, but there are also a lot of funny things about him. (Dale spent a lot of time being the butt of jokes at Moody.)

Dale was the student body president at Moody and I was on a small student leadership team with him. We had a leadership retreat in Montana one year. The school rented a nice bus to take us there. On our trip back from the retreat, they had Buffalo Wild Wings catered at a park for us. We ate and got back on the road. In the final leg of the trip, Dale did the one thing you aren't supposed to do on a bus with a bathroom: unleash Buffalo Wild Wings. When Dale opened the door to the bathroom when he was finished, the smell that left that bathroom was of the devil. As he walked back to his seat, we yelled at him and he owned his smell. He knew what he was doing. It was so bad that we were peeling oranges and shoving the peel into our noses.

Dale. It is an honor to have known you. I didn't know the opportunity would stop so suddenly and, again, I don't know why God took you. I felt you had so much more of an impact to give. But you gave it your all. Until your last breath you glorified your King. You lived His love out in all that you did. You reflected Him in the dialogue you had with people who differed from opinion with you. Your legacy lives on. You've impacted me and you've impacted thousands of others. Your death is not in vain, but in your death we all get to see the legacy you've left. I pray to God I reflect Jesus to the world in even a small percent of the way you did.

I'm crushed by your death but I find so much peace in knowing your suffering is over. He has healed you. You are finally with the One you lived for and have shown all of us. I am so thankful to call you a friend. I love you so much, Dale. Thank you. Thank you for everything. I miss you, I love you, and I'll see you again.

"He will wipe away every tear from their eyes, and death shall be no more, neither shall there be mourning, nor crying, nor pain anymore, for the former things have passed away."

- *Adam Swensen*

I don't think we forget or get numb. I think we remember that we live in a fallen and broken world, and we occupy fallen, broken bodies. And also that death here is only the beginning. This vapor of a moment—a whips as Scripture calls it. I think we remember where we have been and keep our eyes on the prize—Heaven. Jesus. Reunion! Embrace all the emotions as they come. Even when they feel absolutely overwhelming. Cry through them; pray through them; scream through them. And remember He is there. He counts your tears. He knows firsthand the pain you feel. He bears your grief and sorrow. And His promises are sure. His faithfulness is certain. His love for you is certain. Who He is and what He has promised are the ONLY certainty we have. Hold fast to Him. Cling to Him. And you keep processing however you need. Write. Vent here. Call people. Pray. Be still. Move. Do what you feel led to do. But don't disappear. Keep investing in people. Keep telling your Jesus story and Dalez's Jesus story. Share them with zeal and urgency. People need the message you have and the one that led your Dalez HOME! He has all the answers to all the questions now. He IS the New Man. He's alive and thriving in the presence of His king, and he is cheering you on and waiting for you to be in your cloud of witnesses as you enter in to your rest some day! Oh, what a day that will be!! You are so loved and you are prayed for often, sweet one! Keep fighting for and choosing joy. Peace be with you.

- *Tarah Martin*

Testimonials

I enjoy your posts without hesitation I am draw to your words. You are supportive bringing taboo subjects to the forefront. Your uplifting hopeful attitude when Dalez was ill show great strength. Then your rawness when he passed was so embracing. Anyone would read and see that had to be having a better day. We all need to be grateful for each day.

- Daryl Dalcero, FL

You are a living testament for all to see. Even in your darkest hour you never fail to give praise to our God and Savior. It humbles me. You make a difference in people's lives; in my life. May God continue to comfort you and bless you.

- Connie Y. Kannady, OK

Oh, my word! They totally make a difference in my life, friend! I look forward to seeing what you have to say. Even when I have nothing to give back to you when your grief is so evident, your words touch my heart. They make me really consider life: what I'm doing with mine; who I am talking to; what legacy am I leaving; how am I honoring God; how am I reaching out to and praying for those who are hurting. I'd be so sad if you stopped writing (& worried, too!)

Sometimes I can feel the heaviness of your sadness, and yet hear and feel the resolve you have in seeking Jesus and standing firm on his promises.

As we talked about, loss is a familiar thing for me, and I relate to what you have to say, though not on the same level you're writing from. I hope that makes sense.

I feel like you are very intentional about what you write—it's not purposeless rambling.

- *Tarah Martin, OR*

I love reading your posts. My heart breaks for you and your family and it reminds me to pray for you all. Although I have not yet lost someone in my immediate family, I know that death is inevitable so your posts speak to a place in my life that I am not yet in. I appreciate your vulnerability in your grief.

- *Maya Ealy, WA*

From Dale...

God is a god of all things. It's not heretical to say God is in this pen, or that God is in my coffee. Is he literally? Probably not. But is his essence and presence? Is His character revealed in these things? I would say by nature of its existence it would need to be so.

.

If that is true, then all we do reflects something of God. But do we wield that well? Even weapons are creative and powerful, but do they reflect His Goodness?

- *Dale Kompik II*

Other Books by Barbara E. Kompik

Show Me Your Glory: A Mother's Grief for Her Son

Joy in the Mourning

12 Healing Steps Out of the Pain of Abuse

Journey to Wholeness

Finding My Voices: A Fractured Mind After Abuse

Little Boy Blue: Poetry and Prose from Survivors of Abuse

The Sick Little Girl

Losing Dalez

Made in the USA
Middletown, DE
22 November 2019